"An important treatise on a very controversial topic, dealt with sensitivity and respect."

~ **Rabbi Yehoram Ulman**,
Senior Dayan Sydney Beth Din

"Finally, a man who has the courage to say it as it is. This book is not only for women but equally for men. It provides an honest, comprehensive approach to appreciating the role of a woman, her inherent virtues, and her essential role in redemption. A must read!"

~ **Chana Weisberg**,
Editor at Chabad.org,
Bestselling Author

"You take on a daring subject with intelligence, depth, and wit. The style is captivating and the content convincing. I congratulate your courage, research, and commitment to clarify this important subject."

~ **Rabbi Aaron Laine**,
Chief Ashkenazi Rabbi of Beth El Synagogue
Panama City, Panama
Author, *GPS for a Happier Marriage*

"Rabbi Raskin, a pioneer in the field of Jewish outreach; hails from a distinguished rabbinic family, yet his words are assessable, practical, and non-judgmental."

~ **Rabbi Simcha Weinstein**,
Chair of the Religious Affairs Committee at Pratt Institute
Bestselling Author, *Up, Up and Oy Vey*,
Shtick Shift, and *The Case for Children*

"Wherever you stand on women's place in Judaism, it is important to know what the tradition is. In this book by Rabbi Aaron Raskin, a Chabad tzaddik who has only love and honor for Jewish women in his heart, you can hear one authentic voice of that tradition."

~ Maggid Yitzhak Buxbaum,
Author, *Jewish Tales of Holy Women*
and *The Light and Fire of the Baal Shem Tov*

"Rabbi Aaron Raskin provides an insightful and accessible exploration of the role of women in Orthodox Judaism; his book is a compelling read for Jewish women and men alike."

~ Michelle Hodkin,
New York Times Bestselling Author, *Mara Dyer Trilogy*

"One of today's most controversial and heated debates is around the role of women in Judaism. Are they second-class citizens? Why do so many Torah laws seem to exclude women? Rabbi Aaron Raskin, therefore, deserves our deep gratitude for compiling Thank You G-d for Making Me a Woman, *in which he dispels the swirling myths and stereotypes resulting from misguidance or ignorance, demonstrating the woman as the crown jewel she truly is, returning her to the prominence she truly deserves in Jewish life, and appreciating the woman's critical role in building a better world."*

~ Rabbi Simon Jacobson,
Author, *Toward a Meaningful Life*

"In a world of monosyllables, ten-second-attention-spans, and prodigious use of simplistic sloganeering, a lucid exposition by a man extolling the spiritual prowess and beauty of womanhood, is both daring and rare. My colleague, Rabbi Aaron Raskin doesn't engage in inverse polemics between

the sexes. Rather, he blends profundity and wisdom, together with witticism and light-hearted banter, to create a most readable manual on the centrality of womanhood in the Jewish tradition – a much needed primer at a time of superficial machismo and sexism."

~ Rabbi Dr. Laibl Wolf,
Internationally acclaimed lecturer,
Author of the Classic, *Practical Kabbala*

*"*Thank You, G-d, for Making Me a Woman *is the latest book by Rabbi Aaron L. Raskin, the emissary of Chabad Lubavitch for Brooklyn Heights in NYC. It is an engaging, enlightening, and entertaining response to the age-old accusation of traditional Judaism being sexist and misogynous. In very accessible (but definitely not "dumbed-down") language, Rabbi Raskin proves that the exact opposite is true. In Torah Judaism, women are to be treated with the highest respect, being considered closer to the source of holiness than their male counterparts.*

"To cite but one surprising example: you have probably heard that in Islamic Sharia courts, a woman's testimony is valued at only half of a man's testimony. Did you know that in traditional Judaism a woman's testimony carries more weight than that of two males?

"The text is personal and personable, enriched by heartwarming stories and jokes that bring the message home. Thank You, G-d, for Making Me a Woman *is a brief book, but very deep and illuminating. It will definitely change many people's preconceptions and misconceptions about the role of women in the Jewish faith.*

"Thank You, G-d, for making spiritual leaders like Rabbi Raskin."

~ Roy Doliner,
Author, *Sistine Secrets*

THANK YOU GOD FOR MAKING ME A WOMAN

THANK YOU GOD FOR MAKING ME A WOMAN

Empowering Women For The 21St Century

by

Rabbi Aaron L. Raskin

NEXT CENTURY
PUBLISHING

THANK YOU GOD FOR MAKING ME A WOMAN
Empowering Women For The 21St Century

Copyright ©2017 by Rabbi Aaron L. Raskin
All rights reserved.

Published by Next Century Publishing
Las Vegas, Nevada
www.NextCenturyPublishing.com

ISBN: 978-1-68102-219-2
Library of Congress: 2016945760

Printed in the United States of America

DEDICATED TO

All the daughters of Sarah, Rebecca, Rachel and Leah

who light up the world every day with their acts of goodness and kindness

TABLE OF CONTENTS

THANK YOU GOD FOR MAKING ME A WOMAN

PREFACE

In September of 1988, Stephen and Penny Rosen asked me to help initiate a new synagogue in Brooklyn Heights, now called Congregation Bnai Avraham. Stephen is currently the president and Penny is a distinguished board member. A few weeks into the job, a woman cornered me in the hallway after services. Although sporting a veneer of respect, her eyes blazed with the intensity of a woman on a mission and, still new to the job, I didn't have the presence of mind to come up with an excuse and escape while I still had a chance.

"Rabbi," she began, her face intense. "I really enjoy the services here. I enjoy the sermons, the spirit, and the people, but I have a real problem with the way you do some things."

Uh oh, I thought, but outwardly maintained my naïve, welcoming smile.

She crossed her arms. "I am an intelligent, well-educated, professional woman and I want to know why I can't participate in the service. Why can't I be called to the Torah, or counted for the *minyan*, or lead the service? I have a nice voice, too. And this *mechitzah* partition that separates the men and women, what's that all about?" She paused to catch her breath, then jammed her hands on her hips. "And, the biggest problem I have is the blessing 'Thank You G-d…for *not* making me a woman.'" Her eyes bore into mine. "How do you explain that one?"

Her pointed questions caught me off guard, and I doubted I could reach a life vest in time. But, as this was only the beginning of my tenure as a pulpit rabbi—a profession in which other experiences would make this one look tame—I was determined to succeed and, moreover, prove my capability and durability.

I smiled with all the comfort I could muster. "Those are great questions. Let me think about them before I give you some run-of-the-mill answer."

Surprisingly, she agreed and let me go without further fuss.

However, I wasn't off the hook just yet. Finding suitable answers to her queries would prove difficult, not because they weren't there, but because of the advice most of my colleagues offered me instead.

"Listen," they collectively counseled, "you're better off sweeping this whole thing under the rug. There's no way you can win this argument. Forget about it and duck till it blows over."

It wasn't quite the reaction I was expecting. Despite their well-meaning but misguided judgment, I couldn't let it go. Something about this woman's questions had caught hold of me and I wasn't going to move on until I knew more. It took years of research and searching in the dusty crannies of my heritage, but I was finally able to compile the answers I believed would respectfully and satisfactorily answer the woman's complaints.

Many years later, I realized I wasn't only seeking answers for the woman who had stumped me, but also for my wife, my mother, my sister, my daughter, my aunts, my cousins and every other woman who wondered why she was forced behind a partition and couldn't participate in the services. These answers would be a buoy, a beacon, a validation—not only for the uniqueness of women, but also for their supremacy in the spiritual hierarchy. I knew Judaism held women in high esteem; I simply had to prove it.

The book you hold in your hands is the answer to the woman's questions, carefully accumulated from my years of searching for proof that women are also created in G-d's image.

You are right to rhetorically ask: "Why is a man, a Chassidic man and an Orthodox Jew (we are not often noted for progressive thinking), qualified to answer this question? What good are your years of research, if you're missing the one chromosome that would qualify you for this debate? Better concern yourself with prayer three times a day, ensuring your children receive a fine Jewish education and, most importantly, spending time with your wife, instead of locking yourself up in your office to find answers to an almost impregnable topic? Do you think we will cheer your wild undertaking? Daniel was a martyr because he survived being thrown into the lion's den, but we will not celebrate you for jumping in and sticking your head right into the lion's mouth."

> *Why is a man, a Chassidic man qualified to answer this question? If you're missing the one chromosome that would qualify you for this debate?*

Honestly, I don't know why and that could be a topic for another book. But I do believe that this woman specifically asked me these questions for a reason, if only to jumpstart my quest to understand what, if anything, the partition between men and women is really made of.

Philosophically, the sexes agree on most things. For example, it is commendable to give charity, to teach our children about their heritage, to celebrate holidays with loved ones and that a family that prays together, stays together. Most of us are concerned about the friends our children hang out with and the rise in drug and alcohol addiction among teenagers. So why does a *mechitzah* separate us, one family, indivisible, beloved and cherished by G-d?

Tested & Proven

After researching this topic, I learned that the answers to these questions about women have been around since the beginning of time, if not before. In truth, this book is an opportunity for discussion, honest dialogue and, more significantly, insight and growth into the knowledge of the holy Torah and observance of Judaism. I have discussed these answers at lectures and spoken one-on-one with women of different affiliations, most of whom thanked me for my openness in helping them understand and appreciate the awesome role of women and the deeper purpose in the design of their creation. Many have called these answers "eye openers" and have been inspired to more seriously consider their position in society.

> In reference to Albert Einstein's comment that G-d doesn't play dice with the universe, the Lubavitcher Rebbe maintained that, as the creator of the universe, G-d can quite frankly do what He pleases.

Granted, some may not believe in G-d, for reasons ranging from the Holocaust to the unmitigated success of your "evil, wicked neighbor." To quote Rabbi Levi Yitzchok of Berditchev: "The G-d you don't believe in I don't believe in either." As the prophet Isaiah tells us "my thoughts are not your thoughts and my ways are not your ways."[1] Similarly, in reference to Albert Einstein's comment that G-d doesn't play dice with the universe, the Lubavitcher Rebbe maintained that, as the creator of the universe, G-d can quite frankly do what He pleases.[2]

I want to state from the beginning that this is *not* a book about the existence of a Creator or Jewish G-d. However, for you to accept what's written in following pages, you must put all preconceived notions about G-d, spirituality, the afterlife, reincarnation and redemption aside. Some of these topics will fly in the face of your belief system, so please, hang on.

Objective

Throughout the book, I want to demonstrate how, according to the holy Torah, men and women have always been equal. There are even areas where women are held in greater regard than men. The liturgical blessings and teachings of our sages are true, holy and meaningful for every generation, even if the simple translation of the words may seem disparaging. In Judaism, embarrassing another person or even an animal is the worst thing one can do.[3] Therefore, if a statement in the Talmud or Jewish law seems to fall along these lines, we must understand that it was expressed out of love and sensitivity. Even teachings that may seem

---

[1]   Isaiah 55:8

[2]   See Toward A Meaningful Life by Simon Jacobson P. 288 FN. 3.

[3]   Tractate Baba Basra 123A.

derogatory toward women carry the deepest secrets and teachings for all humankind.

The Three Pillars upon which this Book Stands

In writing this book, my approach is based primarily on the teachings of my illustrious teacher and mentor: the Lubavitcher Rebbe Rabbi Menachem Mendel Schneerson. The Rebbe is the Moses of our generation.[4] He is responsible for establishing more than 4,000 Chabad Lubavitch educational and social outreach facilities throughout the world, and was hands down the greatest advocate for women's rights and their role in this generation. At every opportunity, the Rebbe charged and encouraged women to take a leading role in changing the world for the good. Here are three monumental teachings of the Rebbe in this regard:

1. The Midrash[5] states that a kosher woman *oseh*, fulfills the will of her husband. The Rebbe with his vision and admiration for the feminine mystique translated *oseh* as "creates," as in "the kosher woman creates the will of her husband." This acknowledgement and support of the influence of a woman in her house was a paradigm shift in the way the Jewish world would normally understand this verse.

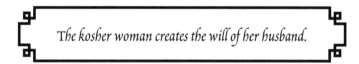

The kosher woman creates the will of her husband.

2. The Rebbe often quoted the Talmud,[6] which states that it was in the merit of the righteous women that our forefathers were redeemed from Egypt. Once again the Rebbe took this quote to the next level by explaining that Egypt is actually a metaphor for all exiles. He emphasized that, just as the Jewish women living in previous exiles were influential in bringing about the redemption, in this final exile, it will be up to the women of our generation

---

4   Tanya Ch. 2
5   Tana Dvai Eliyahu Rabba Ch. 9
6   Tractate Sotah 11B. Midrash Yalkut Shimoni on Psalms remez 795 and on Ezekiel remez 354.

to bring about the coming of Moshiach. Furthermore, the Rebbe enhanced this teaching by drawing upon his formidable knowledge of Kabballah. He quoted the famed kabbalist, the AriZal, who states that our souls today are all reincarnated from generations before.[7] The Rebbe emphasized that the souls of the women of today are the same souls of the women who left Egypt. These feminine souls have returned to this world to facilitate our entire generation's receiving the countenance of our righteous Moshiach.

3. The Rebbe often quoted a verse from King Solomon's Book of Proverbs, "a woman of valor is the crown of her husband.[8]" The Rebbe understood that this did not mean that a wife is an accessory or adornment of her husband, but rather, with the advent of our ultimate redemption, the woman's role will truly topple and outshine the role of men.[9] His view opposes the fact that throughout history women have been mistreated and misunderstood. Attitudes are now changing and consequently so are the roles of women. The Rebbe proved this by highlighting all the great opportunities available to women today, and how women are increasingly taking on leadership roles in both the corporate and private sectors. There are also many areas where women are more proficient and more successful than men.

It is these three teachings, in addition to the Rebbe's other talks and correspondence, that provide the basis from which I have extrapolated and gleaned my insights for this book. It is my fervent wish and prayer that I convey the Rebbe's teachings properly and coherently to salute the great role and responsibility of women in the 21st century.

Story

Some time ago, my wife and I wanted to buy a home, so we went searching from condo to condo until we finally found something in our price range. As Lubavitchers, we wouldn't make this purchase without

---

[7] Shaar Hagilgulim - Introduction 20 and more.

[8] Proverbs 31:10

[9] Hayom Yom - 23 Shvat

first getting a blessing from the Rebbe. Sadly, the Rebbe had suffered a stroke. Though he wasn't able to speak, we knew he would give answers by nodding his head. I called Rabbi Leibel Groner, the Rebbe's secretary, and requested that he ask the Rebbe for a blessing to buy the new condo, then I gave him the address and all the details.

"Before I ask the Rebbe," Rabbi Groner said, "I have a question for you. Does your wife like the condo?"

"What kind of question is that?" I asked. "If I'm calling you, we obviously checked it out together."

"But does your wife like it?" Realizing this was more than a simple question, I asked him to wait a few moments.

"Do you like the condo?" I asked her.

"Not really," she replied.

"Not really," I echoed to Rabbi Groner.

"Not really?" Rabbi Groner responded. "If that's the case, I'm not going to the Rebbe."

"Why not?"

"Because the Rebbe says that the woman is the *akeres habayis*, the mainstay of the home. She has to actually like the home. *It's her home.* You're lucky if she lets you inside that home, because it's hers."[10]

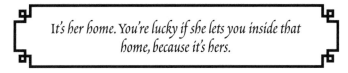

It's her home. You're lucky if she lets you inside that home, because it's hers.

Realizing it was a lost battle, I then asked Rabbi Groner, "Please ask the Rebbe for a blessing to find a new home soon."

He did, and thank G-d we found a new beautiful place a short time later.

---

[10] See Lubavitcher Rebbe's letters, Vol. 17, P. 2. Vol. 19, P. 268.

✷ ✷ ✷ ✷ ✷

I trust I now have your complete attention. I also trust that the rest of this book will enlighten and entertain you, and help you to see that G-D has bestowed the world with a great gift—women.

Yours Sincerely,

Rabbi Aaron L. Raskin

ACKNOWLEDGEMENTS

With praise and thanks to A-mighty G-d,
we are fortunate to present our latest book to the world of readers:
Thank You G-d For Making Me a Woman.

I would like to acknowledge the following people who helped bring this book into fruition. To my Rebbe, Mentor, and Teacher, Rabbi Menachem M. Schneerson whose ideas I try to convey in this book. My grandfather, Rabbi Jacob J. Hecht, who inspired me to be a pulpit Rabbi. Esther Leah Tenenbaum for editing and Chana Minkowicz for typing. Stephen Rosen, the synagogue president of Congregation Bnai Avraham of Brooklyn Heights, who deliberated with me on many of these ideas. Next Century Publishing, Simon Presland, Editor in Chief, for personally taking this book under his wings. Warren and Connie Forman for underwriting this book.

To my wife Shternie, for her love and constant support, and to all of my children for constantly encouraging me to put these ideas into print.

To my parents, Rabbi Benzion and Bassie Raskin for their wisdom. To my in-laws Rabbi Shmuel and Deborah Plotkin for their advice. To my grandmother Rebbetzin Chava Hecht for being a role model and rock for her family.

We hope and pray that words from this book will emanate from our hearts and enter into the heart of each reader, bringing blessing and healing to the world, and helping to usher in the coming of our righteous Moshiach.

CHAPTER 1

What's Wrong with Being a Woman?

A number of years ago, a young man approached me on the street and asked, "Can I come to your synagogue for morning prayers? I need to say *kaddish*, I have *yahrzeit*."

(Kaddish is generally said as a memorial prayer for eleven months after the passing of a parent or close relative. It is also said every year on their yahrzeit, i.e. the anniversary of the day of passing.)

"Sure," I replied. "Come on in."

The next morning, he came to the synagogue bright and early and was one of the first people to arrive for the *minyan*. Later, when I turned around to signal him at the time of reciting *kaddish*, he was already gone. I was puzzled by his disappearance and wondered what could have happened to make him leave before fulfilling his intentions.

The following day, I met him on the street and cut straight to the point. "You came to synagogue because you wanted to say *kaddish*, but then you ran out early. What happened?"

"Rabbi, I can't step foot in your synagogue anymore," he declared.

"Why not?" I was taken aback by his adamancy, searching my mind for any slight I, or anyone else, may have committed.

"Yesterday I was reading the liturgy in the *Siddur,* when I came across the blessing 'Thank you, G-d, for not making me a woman,'" he explained.

23

"How do you expect me to stand in your synagogue while you're saying, 'Thank You, G-d, for not making me a woman' in your prayers?"

The man's question was a resounding echo of the one posed to me by a certain woman in the Fall of '88. This time, however, I was prepared. The answer wasn't short, but I invited him to my office to discuss it further. What follows are many of the points I explained to the man, who greatly appreciated the sensitivity with which I handled his questions.

✳✳✳✳✳

What is the reason behind the seemingly belittling blessing: "Thank you, G-d, for not making me a woman?"

Let's consider a verse from the Torah, which was dictated to Moses by G-d letter by letter, including vowels and cantillations. The Book of Genesis states, "G-d created Adam in his image; man and woman He created him.[11]" One of the most basic questions that bothers the commentators is: How did G-d create man in his image? The answer lies in the text itself—"man and woman He created him."

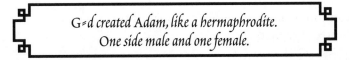

G-d created Adam, like a hermaphrodite. One side male and one female.

The Talmud explains that when G-d created Adam, the first human being, He actually created him with male and female anatomy, like a hermaphrodite,[12] but with one side male and one female. It was only later that day that G-d put Adam to sleep and split him down the back, creating two entities of Adam and Chavah (Eve) who could now turn face-to-face. The Torah calls this first being *"Ha-Adam,"* "the man," because this was the perfect human being. With this word, the Torah underlines that the perfect human is one that has a balance of both male and female qualities. Male tendencies are to be innovative, benevolent and determinantal, in contrast with female tendencies which are to develop potential, nurture, and display genuine humility.

---

11   Genesis 1:27

12   Tractate Brachot. 61A; Midrash Bireshis Rabba 8:1; Rashi on 1:27 Gen. Also see Rashi on Gen. 2:21 that *Mitzsalosav* means side (not rib) as shown in Exodus 26:20.

Along these lines, the Torah explicitly states that a man may not wear the clothing of a woman, nor may a woman wear the clothing of a man.[13] Philosophically, the Torah is teaching us that the role or clothing of a woman is different than but equal to that of a man, and that the role or clothing of a man is equal to but different than that of a woman.[14] If either one changes their dress, neither will end up living the right part.

If humanity can only find perfection in the harmonic balance of man and woman together, and both were truly created in the image of G-d, then why do we say the blessing, "Thank You, G-d, Our G-d, the King of the Universe, *shelo asani isha*, Who has not made me a woman?" This seems blasphemous, considering a woman is also created in G-d's image.

At face value, one can easily surmise that the rabbis who instituted these blessings over 2,400 years ago were misogynists and male chauvinists who really thought very little of women. Even if this were the case, we would point out that this blessing cannot be recited publicly, as the Torah expressly commands us to "love thy neighbor as thyself,"[15] and forbids us from embarrassing our neighbors.[16] Furthermore, the Talmud says that the Torah is so concerned about someone else's feelings, that even the feelings of an animal are not to be overlooked,[17] even for a non-kosher animal.

On top of all that, before Shabbat dinner on Friday night, we make *kiddush* over a cup of wine to acknowledge the holiness of the seventh day when G-d rested from creation. But first we cover the challot,[18] the two white loaves of delicious braided bread, before we begin. Why? Because according to Jewish law, if there is bread and wine in your meal, the blessing over bread should be said before the blessing over wine. In practice this means that we'd have to make the blessing for the challah before blessing the wine. However, there is a mitzvah to make *kiddush* on Friday night to sanctify Shabbat, which must be done before the meal begins. So the Rabbis instructed us to cover the challah when saying *kiddush* so as not embarrass it when its blessing is not recited first.

---

13 Deuteronomy 22:5
14 Toras Menachem, 5742, vol.3 page1660.
15 Leviticus 19:18
16 Ethics 3:11
17 Tractae Bava Basra 123B.
18 Sefer Taamei Haminhagim, no.279; Tur, Ch. 271.

Now I ask you: When was the last time a challah *spoke* to you? When was the last time it piped up from your Shabbat table to complain that the wine was being blessed first? How can an inanimate object feel anything? The point is that the sages are teaching the importance of sensitivity, even when it comes to something inanimate like a challah.

All this considered, if we are so concerned about everyone's feelings, including those of an animal and challah, how, G-d forbid, could the Rabbis embarrass a woman with the blessing of *"shelo asani isha"*— for not making me a woman?

To answer this question, a preliminary understanding of how the Torah views the role of the Jewish woman is needed, as well as an understanding of why we say these blessings every day.

Story

A man goes to his doctor to discuss a very delicate situation.

"My wife is hard of hearing," he explains, "but she doesn't want to get hearing aids. What should I do?"

"This is a very serious situation," the doctor replies gravely. "You need to go home and test your wife's hearing from different distances. When she realizes how close you need to be for her to hear you, she'll get hearing aids on her own."

The man went home to find his wife cooking dinner in the kitchen. He stands thirty feet behind her and asks, "Honey, what's for dinner?"

The wife doesn't respond and the worried husband moves ten feet closer.

"Honey, what's for dinner?" he asks again.

His wife still doesn't respond. He then moves up and stands right behind her so there's no way she can't hear him.

"Honey, what's for dinner?" he almost yells.

His wife turns to him and replies, "For the third time, chicken!"

CHAPTER 2

Ladies First

It is interesting to note that the Torah takes a very clear position concerning women. When Abraham was distraught over his wife Sarah's decision to banish his son Ishmael, who was a bad influence on his younger son Isaac, G-d told him, "Whatever your wife Sarah tells you (to do), you have to listen."[19] From the outset, the first Jewish man was told by G-d that he has to listen to his wife, which is why I am smart enough to listen to my wife, whose name is Sarah. Centuries later, the Talmud[20] makes note of two very learned and pious prophets, Elkana and Elisha, who specifically listened to the advice of their wives. The actions of these men is clear proof that the notion that women, like children, should be seen and not heard is baseless and completely ridiculous.

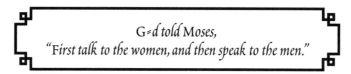

G-d told Moses,
"First talk to the women, and then speak to the men."

Another interesting point pertains to the giving of the Ten Commandments at Sinai. Before one of the greatest moments in history, G-d told Moses, "First talk to the women, and then speak to the men,[21]" meaning ask the women if they are willing to accept my Torah, and only then should you approach the men. G-d knew that the Torah would be

---

[19] Genesis 21:12
[20] Tractate Eruvin 18b; Tractate Brachos, 61A.
[21] Exodus 19:3; Mechilta on loctation; Likkutei Sichos, vol.2, p.577.

safely treasured only if the women were ready to accept it. Additionally, G-d Himself puts "ladies" before "gentlemen."

The Midrash pipes in with a very important comment on the deliberateness of the order G-d chose.[22] The reason G-d turned to the women first at Sinai goes back to the early hours of Adam and Eve's time in the Garden of Eden. G-d told Adam *not* to eat from the Tree of Knowledge, with the instructions to pass on the message to his wife Eve. However, in giving over the message, Adam changed some of the wording, which ultimately led to the serpent's ability to rationalize it and persuade Eve to eat from the tree. After that mishap, G-d knew He had to speak to the women first because they would get it right![23]

The giving of the Torah was not the only time that women would get things right before men in the desert. When it came time to build the holy *mishkan,* the Tabernacle, the women eagerly and readily donated to the building before the men.[24] These few incidents, among others, highlight that the Torah is not embarrassed to say, or celebrate, women and to point out their astute position.

Consider as well in the portion of *Mishpatim* in which the Torah speaks about the laws of slaves.[25] The portion lists three levels of slaves: Canaanite servant, a Jewish male and an *amah Ivria,* or a Jewish maidservant. *Chassidic* philosophy, widely studied as part of the soul of the Torah or the mystical teachings of Torah, explains that these three slaves represent three levels in serving G-d.

The first level represents someone who by nature is rebellious and, therefore, needs to force him/herself to do G-d's will. The next level, that of a Jewish male, is a person who is occasionally inspired to do the right thing, but is still immersed in the desires of the everyday world, and usually must be persuaded to serve G-d. At the highest level, the *amah Ivria* represents someone who passionately desires to serve G-d, without the need for Heavenly inspiration or other outside forces. *Chassidus* unabashedly connects this highest level of service with the *amah Ivria,* a woman.[26]

---

[22] See Midrash Shmos Rabba 28:2.
[23] Likkutei Sichos. Vol. 3, Page.749.
[24] Exodus 25:22
[25] Exodus 21:1-11
[26] See Maamor (discourse): V'ish Ki Yimkor 5714. V'ela Hamishpotim 5738. Likkutei Sichos vol.16 page 257.

Another important and often overlooked point about the Torah's open respect for women is found in the laws of prayer (Amidah). Many of the laws for the *Amidah,* the silent and holiest prayer of the service, are derived from Chana, the mother of the prophet Samuel (more on her later). In tractate Brachos, the Talmud enumerates how many important laws can be learned from Chana:[27]

1. One who prays must direct his/her heart to G-d.

2. One who prays must pronounce the words with his/her lips.

3. It's forbidden to raise ones voice during the (*Amidah*) prayer.

4. A drunkard is not permitted to pray.

5. One who observes a friend doing something improper is obligated to reprove him. (This law is not directed to prayer per say, rather it's a general law derived from Chana.)

Yes, despite all this proof, individuals still feel that women are treated as second class citizens in traditional Judaism. And there's still that unexplained blessing of "Thank You G-d for not making me a woman!"

Adding fuel to the fire, consider that there are eighteen blessings recited first thing in the morning, even before the morning Amidah prayer. These are called the *Birchot HaShachar*[28] and include blessings such as: "Thank You, G-d, who gives the rooster understanding to distinguish between day and night;" the eighteenth one, "Blessed are you, G-d, who removes sleep from my eyes and slumber from my eyelids"; and all of the blessings in-between, for example "the One who prepares the footsteps of our feet" and "straightening the back of those who are bent over." The Code of Jewish Law rightly refers to them as "Blessings of Thanks and Blessings of Praise"[29] as all of them are a positive, showing of gratitude to G-d for His many kindnesses every day. However, toward the end of this list of blessings, there are three consecutive blessings stated in the negative: "Thank You, G-d, for not making me a gentile," "Thank You, G-d, for not making me a slave" and the ad hominem, "Thank You,

---

27   31A
28   Alter Rebbe's Shulchan Aruch, Orach Chaim Ch. 46:1.
29   Ibid.

G-d, for not making me a woman." Why? What did any of them do to be written as a blessing in the negative?

Fortunately, we're not the first to ask this question. The Bach[30] asked the same question in his commentary to the Code of Jewish Law. There he explains the reason these three blessings are written in the negative; in the positive there would only be one blessing, "Thank You, G-d, for making me an Israelite." If one's an Israelite, in the masculine tense, then he's certainly not a gentile, not a (gentile) slave, and definitely not a woman. With this singular, affirmatively written blessing, there would be one blessing for the price of three. But we don't want to make one blessing, we want to make three! Why? Isn't that one blessing nicer than the other three anyway? It's also worded in the positive, so there's no need to worry about disrupting the style of the blessings,[31] or unnecessarily offending anyone.

The Bach explains that Jews are obligated to recite one hundred blessings every day,[32] a tradition started in the times of King David when a terrible plague broke out and killed one hundred people daily. King David beseeched G-d for a way to fix the situation and G-d told him to establish the recital of one hundred blessings a day. From that time onward, Jews look to recite more, not less, blessings daily, and saying one instead of three doesn't help the numbers.

That's all fine and good, but why these three seemingly degrading blessings? What's so special about them that they must be said over other, possibly more positive ones? The Bais Yosef[33] explains in his commentary on the Tor that these three blessings are not about a battle of the sexes or denomination, but rather represent obligations (more on that later). As stated before, it's ludicrous to assert that any rabbi would establish a prayer that is belittling, insulting or diminishing to another person. The Torah believes in the potential and capabilities of every man, woman, or child, Jew and gentile alike; and clearly believes that men and women were created equal, and with their own distinct, respected role in the world.

---

30 Rabbi Yoel Sirkes (1560-1640).
31 Chapter 46
32 Tractate Menochat 43b; Code of the Jewish Law, Orach Chaim Ch. 46.
33 Rabbi Yosef Caro (1488-1575).

As mentioned above, there are some areas of Torah law where women are not only equal to men but considered superior. A prime example is in who determines the soul of a child. The father or the mother? Torah law dictates that if the mother is Jewish and the father is not, the child is one hundred percent Jewish. On the other hand, if the father is Jewish and the mother is not—the child is considered one hundred percent *not* Jewish. The Torah credits the woman with full consideration for what is most relevant to a child's identity—religion and nationhood.

This only heightens the puzzlement around this negative blessing of "*shelo asani isha*." Why are we saying this blessing at all?

Story

While travelling back from teaching at the Ivy League summer Torah study program, a fellow professor told me a story about a young Chassidic man, who wrote a letter to the Rebbe, asking for marital advice shortly after getting married.

The young man wrote that there was a lot of confrontation and shouting going on in his home, and asked the Rebbe's advice on how to properly deal with it before things escalated further.

The Rebbe, through his secretary, replied with a verse from the Torah: "Whatever Sarah (your wife) tells you (to do) hearken to her voice." The Rebbe twice underlined the word *whatever*.[34]

Interestingly, the Rebbe did not tell him to get counseling or try compromising; rather the Rebbe quite clearly stated, "Don't argue, just do what she says!"

> The Torah believes in the potential and capabilities of every man, woman, or child, Jew and gentile alike, and clearly believes that men and women were created equal, and with their own distinct, respected role in the world.

---

[34] Genesis 21:12

31

INTRODUCTION TO CHAPTERS 3, 4 & 5

A Woman's Three Special Mitzvot

To understand the reason behind the blessing, Thank You G-d for *not* making me a woman, it is first important to appreciate the three mitzvot specifically entrusted to women.

When the Torah recounts the first time Isaac meets his future wife Rebecca, it states that he brought her into the tent of his deceased mother, Sarah.[35] Rashi, the tenth century French logician and classic commentator on the Torah, wonders why Isaac would do that, of all things. Surely he should show her to her own tent or perhaps introduce her to his father, instead of taking her around to his mother's tent as soon as they meet. Rashi concludes that Isaac brought Rebecca into Sarah's tent to see if she was like his mother Sarah. He wanted to determine if she had the same kind of qualities that made Sarah so special as the mother of a future nation.

What were the qualities that Isaac was looking for? How would he know if Rebecca measured up to his mother? In the same commentary, Rashi elaborates on three specific miracles that happened with Sarah.

---

35   Genesis 24:67

These miracles departed when she passed, and Isaac wanted to see if Rebecca was righteous enough to bring them back. They were:

1. When Sarah lit Shabbat candles Friday before sundown, they stayed lit until the following Friday.

2. The dough that Sarah kneaded for challah bread was always fresh and plentiful for the many guests that came through her house. (Incidentally, Abraham and Sarah were famous for their hospitality. Strangers traversing the hot desert could rely on them for a warm meal and place to rest before they journeyed on.)

3. A Cloud of Glory hovered over Sarah's tent, implying that the *shechinah,* Divine Presence was at home there. Commentators explain that this refers to the mitzvah of *Mikvah,* family purity.

When Rebecca entered Sarah's tent, these three miracles returned. These miracles reflect a woman's three special mitzvot, or commandments, which are also hinted to in the name *Chana* (mentioned above). In the Hebrew, her name forms an acronym for these mitzvoth.[36]

Cha: Challah

N: Niddah, family purity through Mikvah observance

H: Hadlakat Haneirot, kindling of the Shabbat and Holiday candles (starting from the age of 3).

Chana is not only a pretty name that provides a nifty reminder for the mitzvot of women, but also the name of a very special and holy Jewess. So much so, that her story is read on the first day of the High Holidays, on Rosh Hashanah! Aside from the lessons she taught us in prayer, there is a deeper reason as to why her story, from all those in the holy Torah, was chosen for the first day of Rosh Hashanah.

Chana was barren a long time and every year she would make three annual trips with her husband to the Tabernacle in Shiloh. One particular year, about 2,800 years after the creation of Adam and Eve, she poured out her soul in prayer, begging G-d to have mercy and bless her with a child.

---

[36] Migaleh Amukos Parshas Shlach (begin. 3 Miztvos-17d) based on the Hagohos Maimonidies.

The significance in mentioning Adam and Eve here is that they were created on Rosh Hashanah, and on that very first day of their existence Eve ate from the forbidden Tree of Knowledge and persuaded Adam to do the same. The Midrash says[37] that when Eve[38] screamed and induced Adam to eat this fruit (it was a fig [39] according to some opinions not an apple), she extinguished the light of the world in Adam's soul and essentially ruined the dough of Adam's body and contaminated his blood, rendering him unholy.

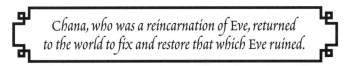

Chana, who was a reincarnation of Eve, returned to the world to fix and restore that which Eve ruined.

Therefore, Chana, who was a reincarnation of Eve, returned to the world to fix and restore that which Eve ruined. In this sense, *Chana* is the antidote to the very first sin that took place on the very first day of the creation of Adam and Eve. *Chana* also optimized the performance of these three mitzvot, as will be elaborated in the next three chapters. So the Talmud[40] specifically states that *Chana* pleaded with G-d for a child and justified her request by asking, "Have I not been scrupulous in lighting the Shabbat candles? Have I not taken dough from my challah? Have I not been meticulous in observing the laws of *mikvah,* family purity? In other words, have I not fixed all that Eve ruined? Why do you still withhold from me a child?"[41]

That year G-d remembered Chana and blessed her with a son who would become the great prophet Samuel, the prophet who merited anointing the first two kings of Israel, Saul and David.[42]

There are 613 mitzvot in the Torah, divided into 248 positive and 365 negative mitzvot. The great scholar Maimonides was famous for his codification and enumeration of the mitzvot. According to his (widely

---

37   Beraishis Rabba end of Ch. 17 Midrash Tanchuma: Beginning of Noach and end of Metzora.

38   Midrash Bereishis Rabba Ch. 19

39   See Rashi on Gen 3:7, the fruit that ruined them now fixed them.

40   Tractate Berachos 31b

41   See Toras Menachem - Vav Tishrei 5727, Ch. 28

42   Ibid 13 Tishrei 5745, Ch. 30

accepted) count, women are obligated in only fourteen less mitzvot than men. For example, women are not obligated to wear Teffilin, put on a Talis, blow or hear the shofar, etc. Women are obligated to keep all negative mitzvot and all positive ones that are not time specific, like know G-d and be in awe of G-d, loves one's neighbor as thyself, eat kosher.[43] From the six hundred and thirteen sacred commandments that G-d gave to the Jewish people, three of them were specifically entrusted to the care and guardianship of women. These three mitzvot are the mitzvah of candle lighting, the mitzvah of Challah, and the mitzvah of family purity.

The next three chapters will examine these three mitzvot in closer detail.

Story

My wife's paternal grandmother, Rebbetzin Chaya Tzirlya Plotkin, related that once during a private meeting with the Rebbe she noted that the Alter Rebbe, the movement's founder and himself a most learned scholar, showed how *gaonim*, brilliant people, could become Chassidim (opponents of the movement long thought it could only appeal to simple Jews). Then his son, the second Rebbe, demonstrated how young people could become Chassidim. The third Rebbe, the Tzemach Tzedek, showed how Rabbis, even of non-Chassidic backgrounds, could become Chassidim. She indicated similar innovations detailing how the fourth, fifth, and sixth Rebbes had expanded the scope of the movement.

"But now," she concluded, "the Rebbe is turning the women into Chassidim."

The Rebbe smiled broadly, even laughed, at her description of him and his plans. He seemed pleased to have been found out that he was opening up the movement—perhaps the first Chassidic Rebbe to ever do so—to the active participation of women.

Sixty years after this encounter and the founding of the Lubavitch Women's Organization, there are over four thousand *shluchot*, women serving as emissaries alongside their husbands in over one thousand communities in some eighty countries.[44]

---

[43] Tractaes Brachos 20b and Kedushin 29a.
[44] Joseph Telushkin, *Rebbe*. HarperCollins, P. 480.

CHAPTER 3

Shabbat Candles: Women, the Forefront of Judaism

From all 613 mitzvot, or commandments in the Torah, why did G-d choose women to safeguard the mitzvah of candle lighting? What deeper meaning does this mitzvah contain that specifically connects it to them?

The Kabbalistic book the *Zohar*, as well as the Midrash,[45] explains that the mitvah of lighting candles can be traced all the way back to Eve in the Garden of Eden. As mentioned, by eating from the forbidden fruit, Eve did not simply extinguish the special light of perfection in Adam but also in the world at large. Therefore, each time Eve, Sarah, Chana and any Jewish woman thereafter lights Shabbat and holiday candles, they reignite that missing light in the world. However, that's the only reason mentioned in the Midrash. The Zohar gives another three answers behind the responsibility of the mitzvah of candle lighting:[46]

1. *Sukkat Shalom,* Covenant of Peace. When women kindle the Shabbat and holiday lights, they bring peace into the world. As written in the liturgy of the Friday night prayers,[47] "Spread upon us the *sukkah* of the cloud of your peace." Only women have the ability to bring down *sukkat shalom* into this world.

---

[45]   Midrash Bereishis Rabba, end of Ch.17

[46]   Zohar Bereishis 48B; See Likkutei Sichos 9 page xii and on, and Toras Menachem Tiferes Levi Yitzchok p. 34.

[47]   The Kehot Siddur, p. 138; The Artscroll Siddur, p. 336.

2. Through lighting the candles, women raise holy children who will become a light unto the world, just like the candles that usher in Shabbat. King Solomon teaches that the flame of a candle represents the study of Torah, and the wax or oil represents the fulfillment of good deeds. The symbolic representation of these candles brings a blessing of light for children of light into the home.

3. A woman brings her husband long life through the lighting of the candles.

The Lubavitcher Rebbe further examined these reasons given by the Midrash and Zohar for women lighting candles.

> He concluded that the reason connected to Eve extinguishing that special light in the world is no longer applicable in present times, because for thousands of years millions of women have lit billions of candles.

There is no question that by now women have surely reignited the candle of the world and brought this special light back. Therefore, the primary reasons must be those stated by the Zohar:[48] peace, holy children and longevity.

Looking at these reasons again:

1. *Sukkat Shalom,* Covenant of Peace.[49] Quoting the verse from the Book of Psalms,[50] the Talmud states that "Almighty G-d brings peace to the borders and He brings creamy fat wheat to satiate the individual." Rhetorically, when is there peace at the borders, i.e. when is there peace in the home? When there is plenty of food to eat, when one is satiated with the creamy wheat and when there's money and food aplenty in the home. As the woman lights the candles, she not only ushers in blessings of peace but also blessings of livelihood. In general, Kabbalah states that the blessing for

---

48   Bereishis 48:B
49   Tractate, Baba Metziah 59A
50   147:14

livelihood, for *parnasah*, is in the merit of the woman, which explains why the sages of the Talmud would tell their students, "Honor your wives in order to become rich."[51] This blessing starts with and is brought into the house when the wife lights the candles.

2. Children. As the Zohar says,[52] lighting these candles gives birth to the candles of the universe, children who will illuminate the universe with their acts of goodness and kindness!

3. Long life or health. The Rebbe explains the words of the Zohar to mean that clearly if a woman brings long life to her husband, surely she will bring long life to herself.[53] As the source of that blessing for others, she is certainly the source of blessing for herself.

Elaborating further, the Rebbe explains how these three reasons essentially represent three very basic needs that most people pray for: children, health and livelihood. By lighting candles, women actually draw down the energy and blessing for these three needs into the home.[54]

Considering these explanations, women are not obligated in the commandment of lighting candles simply because they need to rectify a sin from thousands of years ago. Rather, they truly are the source of energy for the light, holiness and blessing brought into the world when they fulfill this mitzvah. Therefore, the Zohar concludes, a woman should light candles with desire and gladness of heart, appreciating and embracing the power she wields when she lights the candles.[55]

Just to note, a man is allowed to and should light Shabbat candles, if for some reason the woman of the home is absent or he is not married and living alone. The miracle in the candles was granted specifically to women, but who lit the candles in between the time of Sarah's passing and Rebecca's entry into her tent? Abraham. However, the miracle of the

---

51 Tractate, Baba Metziah ibid; Alter Rebbe's Shulchan Aruch, laws of Onaah, law 32.
52 Ibid.
53 Likkutei Sichos Vol.9, P. xii.
54 Toras Menachem Tiferes Levi Yitzchok, Bereshis, P. 35.
55 Ibid.

candles burning from week to week is not mentioned during this time because only Sarah, the woman, was given this added power.[56]

Furthermore, Chassidic philosophy explains that every year on Rosh Hoshanah at the time of the blowing of the *shofar*, the ram's horn, G-d brings forth a new light and energy into this world, which is greater than the year before. This translates into granting each individual a greater potential to become better and to accomplish even more than the year before. The same idea applies every Friday when a woman lights Shabbat candles. She is not simply repeating the same action week after week. Rather, each time she lights the candles, she elicits a new and greater light for blessings for children, health and livelihood.

The Zohar[57] says that the word *ner*, candle, has the *gematria*[58] of 250. Why is this significant? As stated in the introduction to our chapter, of the 613 mitzvot, there are 248 positive commandments. Our sages teach that each commandment should be done with *ahavah* and *yirah*, or the love and awe of G-d. The Alter Rebbe explains in his masterpiece the Tanya that when a person fulfills a commandment without proper holy intent and emotion, i.e. love and awe of G-d, then the mitzvah is like a bird without wings,[59] one that is grounded in this world and cannot soar above.

Combining these concepts, the Rebbe teaches that when a woman lights the *candles* Friday afternoon, she brings this light of Torah and mitzvot into her home, inspiring her husband and children to fulfill the 248 positive mitzvot with love and awe of the Creator.[60] Women are also generally considered more emotional than men, but in ways that are to their benefit. Women use these emotions to infuse the mitzvot they do with love, light, joy and excitement. This approach to mitzvot creates the wings that allow their mitzvot to soar to heaven, and they inspire their husbands and children to do the same.

---

[56]   Likkutei Sichos vol.15, p.172.

[57]   Zohar II, p. 166B.

[58]   Each letter of the Hebrew alphabet has a numerical equivalent called a *gematria*. These numbers are often used in mathematical equations to derive deeper meanings into words and phrases. See Letters of Light written by the author.

[59]   Chapter 40 (near end)

[60]   Sefer Hasichos 5752, pp. 302 and 356.

It's written in the Zohar that, "Shabbat blesses the entire week."[61] In essence, the mitzvah of Shabbat candles underscores the role of Jewish women as the forefront of all that is Jewish and holy. By lighting candles eighteen minutes before sunset, the woman is the first to usher in and sanctify Shabbat; lighting the candles comes before evening prayers and before her husband's recital of the Kiddush. The woman establishes the holiness and greatness of Shabbat, inspires the children with her love and awe of G-d and teaches her family how to do all 248 positive commandments with sincerity and emotion up to an hour earlier than a man.

In truth, the candles are only a one example of how women come first because Jewish history is brimming with similar examples. As explained previously, when it was time for the giving of the Torah, G-d's most cherished treasure, G-d instructed Moses to speak to the daughters of Israel about accepting and upholding it before the men. Four months later, when it was time to build the *mishkan*, a sanctuary for G-d in the dessert, the women stepped up first to donate of their time and possessions. Only after the women gave did the men follow suit. This example shows that women are not only first when it comes to spiritual things, but also in material things as well.

The reverse was also true when the Jews sinned in the desert by building the golden calf.[62] Rabbi Tanchuma states that Aaron instructed the men to go home and get their wives' jewelry for the calf's making because he was really trying to procrastinate and buy Moses more time to get back and keep the people from committing this grievous sin so soon after receiving the Torah. When the men went home and asked their wives for their jewelry, they adamantly refused to hand anything over.[63] This story clearly shows that women are not only the impetus for positive and holy things, but also know how and when to say *no* to things that are negative and unholy.

> *When the men asked their wives for their jewelry,*
> *they adamantly refused to hand anything over.*

---

[61]   Zohar II page 63b and 88a.
[62]   Sefer Hasichos 5752 Vol. I, P. 299.
[63]   Tanchuma 21; Rashi on Exodus 32:2

*An additional aspect of candle lighting is understood through the Rebbe's special request that women give *tzedakah*, money to charity, before lighting candles.[64] (As an aside, on another occasion, the Rebbe spoke about the importance of women placing a *tzedakah* box in the kitchen, preferably on or nailed to the wall, so that it specifically becomes part of the kitchen.[65] The Rebbe said that doing so would actually give a better flavor to the food, in addition to all the other blessings it would bring into the home. Of course, this should be done regardless of who runs the kitchen. Personally, I believe that affixing it to the wall makes the entire house a *tzedkah* box, and thereby a vessel for G-d's blessing. Because G-d's blessing is infinite, the amount we receive depends on the size of the vessel we create. If you have a small vessel, you can only get a little blessing; if you have a big, big vessel, you're able to acquire much more. Putting the *tzedakah* box on the wall of the kitchen, the "energy source" of the home, brings the *tzedakah* box onto all four walls of the house, making it a giant charity box.)

In regard to why giving charity before candle lighting is so important, the Rebbe once wrote that from the 613 mitzvot in the Torah, only a select few are called a "remembrance." For example, the fifth of the Ten Commandments is to, "Remember the Shabbat and keep it holy." In this case, the verse specifically says to "*remember* the Shabbat day."[66] This terminology is also used in reference to the Exodus from Egypt, "*Remember* the going out of Egypt.*"[67] A third example is the most important Jewish event in history, when G-d gave the Torah on Sinai, making the Jewish people his nation and entrusting them with the Ten Commandments and all the laws of the Torah. The verse says, "*Remember* what happened to you at *Chorev* [Mount Sinai]."[68] As something that defined thousands of years of history, does G-d really need to specify this as a remembrance?

Every mitzvah of the Torah is important, but throughout the day people are preoccupied with earning a living, eating, drinking, sleeping and other material pursuits, so it is easy to forget the more spiritual things that seem less relevant to us on a day-to-day basis. Therefore, the

64 Kitzur Shulchan Aruch 75:2; Likkutei Sichos, Vol.16 page 577 and Vol. 24 page 298.
65 See Toras Menachem 5748 vol. 4 pages 343,388.
66 Exodus 20:8
67 Deuteronomy 16:3
68 Ibid. 4:10

Torah puts a specific emphasis on these three mitzvot; Shabbat, Passover (Exodus from Egypt) and Shavuot (giving of the Torah).

Essentially, G-d is saying,

> I know you're busy; I know you're doing important things, but remember when Friday evening comes, you've got to stop all your work and keep Shabbat. I know all year you can eat cookies and cake and bread, and all these wonderful things that might have *chometz* in it, but when Passover comes, remember it. And all year, you're involved in all these other responsibilities, but today is Shavuot, the day you became a nation unto Me, the day I appeared to you at Sinai and gave you the Ten Commandments. You've got to stop working, you've got to remember what it's all about.

Interestingly, the mitzvah of lighting candles is included within these three remembrances, as women kindle candles before Shabbat and holidays, such as Passover and Shavuot. The act of lighting candles reinforces the remembrance. It reminds us that this is an important day, made even more important by the acts we do to celebrate it. As the candles themselves are a remembrance of the holy day, giving *tzedakah* serves as a reminder to light the candles. From the various mitzvot, *tzedakah* can be very easy because you simply need to drop a few coins into the charity box and you're done.

However, *tzedakah* is a very powerful mitzvah, too. The Alter Rebbe explains in Tanya[69] that most mitzvot are connected to a specific limb of the body; feet carry a body to shul, a mouth eats kosher food and prays, the arm wears tefillin and the mind studies Torah. *Tzedakah* is one of the few mitzvot that incorporate the entire body in its fulfilment. Why? Because every part of you worked hard for that money; you sweated, you cried, you bled to earn it, and instead of using it for personal benefit, you're giving it to someone in need. When you give *tzedakah,* it's as if you're giving of your entire essence to help someone else. When the woman gives charity before lighting candles, she signals this idea to the entire house.

---

[69] Chapter 37

Instructions and Blessings for Shabbat Candles

Starting at the age of three until marriage, <u>women</u> and <u>girls</u> light one candle. Post-marriage, women light (at least) two candles. Some add an additional candle for each child: e.g., a woman with three children lights five candles.

If no woman (over the age of bat mitzvah) is present in the home, a man should light the candles.

On Fridays, light the candles <u>18 minutes before sunset</u>—and under no circumstances later than sunset! The times fluctuate based on date and location— (On holidays [other than Yom Kippur] that do not coincide with Shabbat, one may light the candles after sunset, using an existing flame.)

The Procedure

- Place <u>several coins in a charity box</u>.
- Light the candles. Place the lit match on designated surface.
- <u>Extend your hands</u> over the candles, draw them inwards three times in a circular motion, and then <u>cover your eyes</u>.

Recite the following Blessing:

Baruch a-ta A-do-noi E-lo-hei-nu me-lech ha-o-lam a-sher ki-di-sha-nu bi-mitz-vo-sav vi-tzi-va-nu li-had-lik ner shel Sha-bat ko-desh.

Translation: Blessed are you, L-rd our G-d, King of the universe, who has sanctified us with His commandments, and commanded us to kindle the light of the Holy Shabbat.

For Holidays Recite:

Baruch a-ta A-do-noi E-lo-hei-nu me-lech ha-o-lam a-sher ki-di-sha-nu be-mitz-vo-sav vi-tzi-va-nu li-had-lik ner shel Yom Tov.

Baruch a-ta A-do-noi E-lo-hei-nu me-lech ha-o-lam she-he-che-ya-nu vi-keeyi-ma-nu vi-hi-gee-an-u liz-man ha-zeh.

Translation: Blessed are you, L-rd our G-d, King of the universe, who has sanctified us with His commandments, and commanded us to kindle the light of the Holiday.

Translation: Blessed are you, L-rd our G-d, King of the universe, who has granted us life, sustained us and enabled us to reach this occasion.

- Now, while your eyes are still covered, it is an auspicious time to pray for your heart's desires. The custom is to pray for children who will be upright and G-d-fearing, and for the a world filled with peace and the coming of Moshiach. Take the time also to pray for others who need blessings and good health.
- Uncover your eyes, gaze at the candles, and then greet everyone with blessings of a good Shabbat or holiday.

(www.chabad.org/Shabbat)

Another approach is connected to the first answer given by the Zohar as to why women are obligated to light Shabbat candles. Women light candles to rectify the sin of Eve, who extinguished the light of the world, and lighting Shabbat candles rectifies this. The same idea is true with charity, about which the Talmud proclaims, "Great is charity."[70] Charity is considered so great because it literally saves lives.[71] Both of these mitzvot, charity and lighting candles, are about saving lives and bringing more life, light and vitality into the whole world.

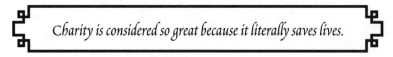

Charity is considered so great because it literally saves lives.

Although kindling Shabbat candles was generally only done by married women, the Rebbe strongly encouraged young girls from the age of three (or even younger, if they can) to start lighting candles.[72] These young girls, who are innocent of sin, bring an immense light and positive energy into the world when they light candles. Just before they do so, their mother gives them a few coins to give to charity, reminding them of the importance of this mitzvah.

The Yalkut Shimoni states that G-d promises, "If you maintain the Shabbat candles, I will show you the candles of Zion."[73] Simply said, lighting Shabbat candles ushers in the ultimate Messianic redemption. As mentioned earlier, the Talmud reveals that it was in the merit of the righteous women that our forefathers[74] were redeemed from the land of Egypt. About this, the AriZal explains that the souls of this generation are a reincarnation of those souls, and therefore, the women of this generation will once again bring about the redemption for their people.[75]

---

[70] Tractate, Baba Basra 10A.

[71] Proverbs 10:2

[72] Likkutei Sichos 15 page 170. Toras Menachem 5749 vol.4 page 378.

[73] Midrash Yalkut Shimoni, Bhaalsocho Remez 719; Tanchuma Buber Noach Ch.1

[74] Shaar Hagilgulim - Introduction 20 and more.

[75] There are 6,000,000 general souls, and each one of these are divided into 6,000,000 additional souls. Furthermore, an individual soul can have multiple bodies, and all of these bodies will be resurrected following the arrival of the messiah. See Tanya, Ch. 2 and 37; Igerret Hakodesh Epistle 7 and Beurim Lepirkei Lepirrike Avot, p. 506.

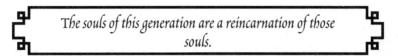

The souls of this generation are a reincarnation of those souls.

It is well accepted that after a woman recites the blessing on the candles, she keeps her eyes covered to have a private, intimate moment with G-d. Then she can ask for anything she wants and needs, and should also ask for the light of Moshiach; then the entire world will be blessed with a covenant of peace. May this all unfold now!

Story

The Rebbe and his wife, Rebbetzin Chaya Mushka, were avid readers, and once during a trip to the library the librarian noticed the name on the Rebbetzin's card.

"Your name is Schneerson," she said. "Are you related to the famous Rabbi Schneerson?"[76]

The Rebbetzin humbly responded, "Yes, that's my husband."

The librarian became teary-eyed, and, startled by her reaction, the Rebbetzin inquired why she was upset.

"I'm not religious, but I had a problem," the librarian said. "I've been married for many years, but have not been blessed with children. A friend suggested that I go to the Rabbi for dollars on Sunday and ask him for a blessing for children. So I went to the Rebbe and he told me that I should start lighting Shabbat candles."

"Nu? Do you light candles?" the Rebbetzin pressed.

"Yes, every week, but I still don't have children."

The Rebbetzin considered her response a moment and then kindly asked, "What time do you light the candles?"

"Every week at 6:30, when my husband comes home from work. Then we eat the Shabbat meal together."

---

[76] Told to me by Avraham Bistritzky.

The Rebbetzin responded softly and urgently, "It's very important to light the candles *before* sunset. There's a mitzvah to light Shabbat candles, but there's also a mitzvah to light the Shabbat candles at the right time. If you light the candles before the sun sets, I'm sure that my husband's blessings will come into effect, and you will be blessed with a child."

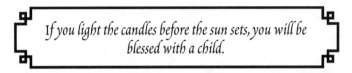

If you light the candles before the sun sets, you will be blessed with a child.

The happy ending to this story is that the woman began to light Shabbat candles at their proper time, and less than ten months later she gave birth to her first child.

This story is poignant because it shows that lighting Shabbat candles is not just a blessing for children already born, but also a blessing to beget children. It's also a blessing to find your soul mate, and the blessing for many other good things. We are told that those who behold this mitzvah to light the Shabbat candles, will truly see the lights of Zion with the coming of Moshiach. Amen. So may it be!

CHAPTER 4

Challah: The Bread Of Faith

The Midrash teaches that Adam is like challah because G-d "kneaded" his form from the four elements of the world.[77] In this vein, the Midrash goes on to say that because Eve destroyed and tarnished the challah of the world by persuading Adam to eat from the forbidden fruit, she needs to fix this by giving challah, a portion of her dough to G-d. What exactly does all this mean?

In more Kabbalistic terms, before the sin of the Garden of Eden, G-d was palpably felt everywhere.[78] Eve sinned by eating fruit from the Tree of Knowledge, then giving it to her husband to eat. Through this action, she separated the perfect harmony of holiness and physicality that existed in the Garden of Eden—she separated heaven from earth. Therefore, in order to restore the world, to fix the world, to repair the damage of the first sin, she needs to elevate the world and bring it closer to G-d. She needs to reconnect heaven and earth. She does this through the mitzvah of challah.

Many people think that challah is only the delicious brown braided loaves we eat Friday night. In truth, challah is the piece of dough you separate and consecrate to G-d when making challah. When the Holy Temple stood in Jerusalem, these pieces would be given to the *kohanim*,

---

[77]   Jerusalem Talmud Shabbat 2:6; Breishis Rabba 14:1
[78]   Torah Ohr 5c and on.

the priests who served for the Jewish people in the Temple.[79] This custom is still practiced today but with a slight variation. The piece of dough is burned until it is inedible, because the Holy Temple no longer stands; no one is allowed to partake of this consecrated piece of dough.

On a deeper level, flour is made up of many fragmented particles and the only way they can be brought together is when they are bound by something like water. By adding water to flour, the flour becomes one, united.[80] Flour represents the multitude of splintered or fragmented physical objects in the grandeur of the universe. Torah knowledge is compared to water, so adding water to flour is a physical representation of bringing spiritual knowledge into the physical world, thereby making it one with G-d. So challah isn't just a homemade treat, it's also a mitzvah and melding of the spiritual with the physical.

With this in mind, we can appreciate the teaching of the Midrash: "Whoever observes the mitzvah of challah is considered to have nullified the idols. However, one who nullifies the mitzvah of challah is considered to be as if he had sustained the idols."[81]

At first glance, it seems odd to connect the mitzvah of challah to idols, especially as this teaching is speaking about their nullification and sustention. Even their reference seems to imply that they exist and yet we know that G-d specifically commanded in the second of the Ten Commandments that one not worship idols.[82] Maybe it should have stated that one who *observes* the mitzvah of challah is considered to have denied the existence of idols, but one who *does not observe* the mitzvah of challah is considered to acknowledge their existence? And where did these idols come from anyway?

In actuality, the Midrash is not speaking of idols that physically exist; rather it's referring to the observer himself,[83] i.e., the person who works his field, plows, sows, harvests, grinds the wheat to flour, makes delicious bread, then says, "I did all this. It's my power. It's my ingenuity. It's my success. I am the master of my own fate." This person credits his hard

---

[79]   Rambam laws of Bikurim 5:1
[80]   Sefer Mamorim Parsha Shelach 5729
[81]   Midrash Vayikra Rabba 15:6
[82]   Exodus 20:3
[83]   Likkutei Sichos Vol.18 P. 184.

work and the natural elements for the food he eats, forgetting entirely about G-d. Even if he believes that G-d created nature, he still thinks that G-d stepped aside and handed the laws of nature over to, well, nature.

The mitzvah of challah is not only a negation of this erroneous and idolatrous thinking, but also gives praise to and celebrates the benevolent G-d who has allowed the natural cycle to provide our bread. This is why before braiding the dough for ourselves a small piece is removed and consecrated for the true Giver. (As an aside, the mitzvah of challah should not be confused with the mitzvah of *tzedakah*. There a person thinks, *I worked hard. I made a lot of money, but now I feel bad for somebody, so I'll give him ten percent of my earnings. It's my hard-earned money that I'm giving the other person.* The mitzvah of challah implies the opposite. Here the person recognizes that he never owned the dough to begin with because it's all G-d's as nature has no power to give on its own.)

Returning to the concept of idolatry, idolatrous beliefs claim that G-d gave power to the Zodiac, to the planets, to the sun and moon, all of which provide warmth, direction, inspiration or light to the world. Really, any of the stars or planets in the cosmos are nothing more than an axe in the hands of a woodchopper,[84] all are tools in the hands of the A-mighty with a set purpose in the world. The mitzvah of challah negates the notion that any aspect of nature can have any power on its own, which is why the Midrash says that if, for some reason, you neglect the mitzvah of challah, even accidentally, you sustain these idolatrous beliefs.

It may seem unfair that the Midrash is so harsh in this assertion, but it doesn't give you leeway in forgetting something right in front of you. When you place G-d before you all day, every day, then you will never forget from where your bread comes.

This leads to another interesting point. Ezekiel the Prophet tells us in regard to Messianic times, "The first of your dough shall you give to the Kohen," and by doing so "You will bring G-d's blessing into your home.[85]" In essence, Ezekiel is saying that the mitzvah of challah is so great that it brings G-d's blessings into the entire home, which is a pretty

---

[84] See Rambam Laws Of Avodas Kochavim Chap.1
[85] Ezekiel 44:30

big blessing in return for just one small piece of dough. Perhaps there's something more to this verse that gives deeper insight into the greatness of the mitzvah of challah?

Rereading the verse in its original Hebrew, the word *auris* is used, usually translated as dough. *Auris,* however, can also mean a crib or a bed. Using this translation, the verse translates to mean that from the time a child wakes up in his crib, he is already consecrated, a *terumah,* to G-d.[86] The implication of this is that from the moment a child wakes up in the morning, before he can even start his day, we teach him to dedicate his strength and energies to the service of G-d. This is done by the recital of the *Modeh Ani* prayer, said before getting out of bed, which thanks G-d for returning our souls each day. It also thanks G-d for having faith in us mortals to fulfill His will by making this world a better, more productive place and an edifice G-d can call His home and garden. This gratitude and acknowledgement blesses the entire house; like challah, you take from the first and best of what you have and give it to G-d.

(Just to note: This is why many Jewish day schools set their schedules so that all Judaic studies, Talmud, Jewish Law, Chassidic Philosophy, are studied in the morning, and general study subjects, like math, history and the sciences, are relegated to the afternoon. In this way, they dedicate the first and best of their energies to G-d. When G-d sees that you make Him your priority, G-d then says, "I will make you my priority," thusly "You will bring G-d's blessing into your home.")

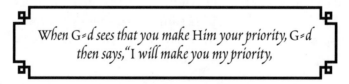

When G-d sees that you make Him your priority, G-d
then says, "I will make you my priority,

All of this is why the mitzvah of challah was given to women. While it fits to say that women must rectify the sin of Eve who destroyed the first challah of the world, like candle lighting, its application is weak if only because millions of woman have been rectifying this misdeed for thousands of years. No doubt, they already fixed that mistake. Rather, entrusting this mitzvah to women has more to do with the later translation

---

86   Likkutei Sichos Vol.8, P. 308.

of the verse, which places women in a more positive light. Only a mother has the ability to infuse her child with a love and dedication for G-d from the moment the child is born and placed in the crib, as a father does not have that same relationship, that same impact on the child. From the moment the child is put in a crib, its mother teaches and inspires it to always give the first and the best of what he has to G-d.

This brings us to a very curious and startling situation. Today, in many communities, there are Jews who practice a lifestyle degrading and unsavory to their heritage. It is difficult to fathom that the people who stood at Mount Sinai—and the souls of every Jew in every generation until the end of time were there at least in spirit, if not in body—and unanimously accepted to uphold and keep the laws of the Torah, could have among them those who live a life foreign to the teachings of the Torah. How could these people so readily forget the revelations and commitments made at Mount Sinai?[87]

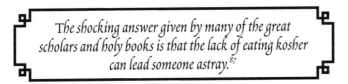

The shocking answer given by many of the great scholars and holy books is that the lack of eating kosher can lead someone astray.[87]

In a broader sense, the mitzvah of challah is not only a consecration of the dough you make, but also a reminder to make sure that all the food in your house is appropriate before G-d. The importance of the mitzvah of kosher can be summed up in one familiar phrase: you are what you eat.

This point is highlighted in the familiar answer given as to why Jews don't eat non-kosher animals. Most carnivorous animals that aren't kosher, such as bears or lions, are ferocious predators that do not hesitate to attack and rip their prey apart. As the impulse to attack others and rip them apart physically, spiritually and emotionally is something we want to stay well away from, we don't eat animals that have that in their nature. The same idea can also be understood on a much simpler level; heavy, fatty foods and alcoholic beverages make it much more difficult for the mind to think clearly, whereas cleaner foods contribute to a cleaner and clearer mind.

---

87   Likkutei Sichos Vol.13, P. 260.

Recipe For Challah Bread

---

5 pounds sifted all-purpose flour (or SPELT)

2 ounces fresh yeast

2 tablespoons coarse salt

4 1/4 cups warm water (add an additional 1/4 cup for softer dough)

3/4 cup oil

1 1/3 cups sugar

5 egg yolks

Dissolve the yeast in 1 cup of warm water and add 1 tablespoon of sugar. Stir. When bubbles rise, the yeast has activated. In your mixer, combine the salt, 2/3 of the flour, oil, sugar, yolks, water and the activated yeast last. Set the machine on medium for 12 minutes. When you see the dough begin to form, add the remaining flour into the mixer and continue mixing.

Transfer the dough to a very large well-greased bowl, cover with plastic and allow to rise in a warm spot for 2 to 3 hours or until double in bulk. (Optional: punch dough down after 1 hour and let rise again)

Separate the challah and make a blessing. Remove a piece of dough the size of a babies fist (approx. 2oz.) and burn it in the oven until it becomes inedible.

Before separating the challah, the following blessing is recited:

Baruch a-ta A-do-noi E-lo-hei-nu me-lech ha-o-lam asher kid-e-sha-nu b'mitz-vo-sav v'tzi-vanu le-haf-rish challah.

Translation: Blessed are You, L-rd our G-d, King of the universe, who has sanctified us with His commandments and commanded us to separate challah.

(When making Challah dough with water and with 3 lbs. 11 oz. of flour or more one is required to recite the above blessing before separating the dough.)

Six-Braided Challah Divide the dough into 4 parts to make 3 large challahs and 6 small challah rolls. To make a six-braided challah, divide one large part into 6 small sections. Roll each section out to a 12 inch strand. Connect the strands on top and place two strands to the right, two to the center and two to the left. Pull the center left strand up and the center right remains down. Grab the inner center right strand and the inner left strand and pull the outer left strand under. Pull the center left strand up and the center right strand down and then grab the center right strand and the inner right and pull the outer right strand under. Pull the center left strand down and the center right strand up and grab the inner center left and the inner left and pull the outer left strand under. Repeat "down and up and under" til you reach the end. Then take your six strands and tuck them neatly under the challah.

After you have formed your challahs allow them to rise for 20 minutes in greased baking dishes. Paint the challahs with beaten egg yolks and sprinkle with poppy or sesame seeds. Bake in a preheated 400 degree oven for the first 15 minutes then, reduce to 350 degrees for another 30 to 45 minutes.

(For more info www.Chabad.org/Challah)

As much as these ideas apply on a physical level, they apply on a spiritual level as well. The *neshama*, the soul, is sent down to the body against its will. Having spent its pre-earth life in the Garden of Eden basking in the glory and perfection of G-d, it's a tough sell getting the soul to agree to stay in the body. However, it is told that its descent to this world is in order to acquire a greater ascent. Once it sees how much an individual soul can do, once it sees how great the potential to turn darkness into light, it's hooked.

Now comes the real work. How does the soul fight the darkness? Through prayer, Torah study, *tzedakah* and good deeds. To do this however, the soul needs strength so that it can blaze a trail through this cold and dark world. By feeding it kosher, the soul becomes stronger. In contrast, when it is fed non-kosher foods the soul is smothered and suppressed, thus becoming disoriented and forgetting the goals that it was sent to earth to accomplish. Giving the soul non-kosher foods, weighs it down and makes it harder for the soul to fight against the animalistic urgings and cravings of the body.

This is why the woman's role of establishing a kosher home is so important for the spiritual health of her children. G-d knows the strength and capability of a woman, He knows that he can trust her, and therefore has endowed her with this sacred task.

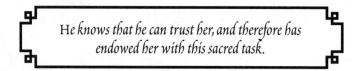

He knows that he can trust her, and therefore has endowed her with this sacred task.

Story

When I first moved to Brooklyn Heights more than twenty five years ago, a young man came to me because he was trying to keep kosher.

"But my wife is not letting me," he complained.

"That's odd," I responded. "Why not?"

"Well, Rabbi, I have a young son, whom we need to make sure gets a lot of protein. The local stores don't sell kosher meat, and the only baby food with protein is not kosher."

"Tell me the truth," I insisted, "You say that you are kosher, but your wife does not keep a kosher house. Are you truly kosher?"

"In the house, I keep kosher," came his firm reply.

"And out of the house?"

"Well, outside the house is not as simple. There aren't kosher restaurants where I work, so I don't always keep kosher then, but at home I'm definitely, one hundred percent kosher. And at home is where my wife is feeding my son not-kosher food. What am I supposed to do?"

I was sure there was something more to this issue than just baby food. "Tell me, do you do other religious things that bother your wife?"

The man thought a moment then answered. "Now that you ask, I go to synagogue Saturday mornings, which upsets my wife, too."

"Why is that?"

"Because I usually take care of the baby Saturday morning, but now that I'm in synagogue, I don't spend that time with him anymore."

"Anything else?" "I used to wash the dishes Saturday morning, too," he conceded.

By now I had a pretty good idea of what the crux of the problem was. "Listen," I said to the man, "Women are very, very smart. They don't believe in bluff. If you're an honest, straight person, your wife will respect you; if she detects falsehood, she won't respect you.

"You're telling me that in the house you're kosher, but then you go to work and eat non-kosher *(treif)*. Your wife says, 'you're not kosher, so what do you want from me? You eat what you want when you want but I have to schlep kosher food into the house. You make me do all the work.' When your wife sees that you are as kosher outside the house as you are inside the house, I guarantee you she will also keep a kosher home. Secondly, she's correct about Saturday morning. Now you run to shul and you leave your child with her. Take the child with you to shul. Let your wife sleep an extra hour Saturday morning, and make sure you do the dishes. Don't use Judaism as an excuse to *not* do these things."

Shortly after our meeting, the man turned my advice into action and his wife came to respect his choices and join them, too. Thank G-d he listened really well, and today the family is kosher and Shabbat observant and recently made Aliya to Israel.

CHAPTER 5

Mikvah: Bringing Passion Back into Your Marriage

In the year 2000, the famous author and speaker John Gray, who wrote the book *Men are from Mars, Women are from Venus,* came to our synagogue Congregation Bnai Avraham in Brooklyn Heights to speak. We had recently completed construction on our *mikvah,* ritual bath, and I asked him if he would like a tour of the facilities. He said yes and we were soon showing him around the newly built shower rooms and *mikvah* pool.

At the end of the tour, he turned to me with a big smile. "Wow, this is great! I love the *mikvah.*"

"You love the *mikvah?*" I stammered, confused. To be honest, that's not the usual reaction men have.

"Truth is," he replied, "*mikvah* is the greatest secret for a happy marriage."

Now I was even more confused. "How do you know that?" He took a deep breath, then exhaled. "When couples come to me and say, 'John, we're not getting along,' I immediately tell them to separate for a week. They must sleep in separate rooms and can't touch each other at all. They must simply talk and communicate verbally. Then the couple is supposed to come back in about a week to discuss their problems. Usually, the couple comes back a week later, and says, 'John, we're so sorry, we couldn't stay apart for more than two or three days; we had to get back together. I hope you can still work with us.' Of course, that was my objective because absence makes the heart grow fonder. So I really love the concept of *mikvah* because the laws of *mikvah* state that men and women should separate, and through that separation they develop a longing to be with each other. After the woman immerses in the *mikvah*, they get back together, and really unite."

"Maybe you should put it in your next book," I suggested.

"Really, rabbi," he replied, "I'm not a rabbi nor am I an authority on *mikvah*, so I can't do that. But one-on-one, I figured I could tell you."

The idea that "absence makes the heart grow fonder" is a concept that the Talmud spoke of over 1400 years ago. As Rabbi Meir would say, "Why is it that the Torah says that a woman who is menstruating (a *niddah* in Hebrew) should separate from her husband?' So that she should be beloved by him in the same way as when she first entered into the marriage canopy, on their wedding day."[88]

It is important to understand where *niddah* or menstruation originally comes from and why it's something that so strongly impacts our conduct in marriage today. The Talmud[89] teaches that after Adam and Eve sinned in the Garden of Eden, G-d brought many curses upon them. Upon Adam He brought the curses of the ground, which would produce loathsome weeds and thorns and only by the sweat of his face and much toil would he eat bread. Adam was also cursed with the inevitable death to man upon earth and weakness after intimacy, to mention a few.[90] Upon Eve were brought the curses of menstruation, pregnancy, labor pains and child rearing, to mention a few. In other words, menstruation is an abnormal state that goes against the grain of creation because G-d didn't include it in His original design. It follows logic that because this loss of blood came about because of sin, it would automatically make the person who menstruates impure, as this blood comes from an impure source.

In truth, menstruation is not specifically a punishment, per se, but rather a reaction to the Jewish state of being. The Jewish people are a holy people, a holy nation, and holiness cannot tolerate something that is unholy, so once a month the body ejects and banishes all unholy toxins

---

[88] Niddah 31b

[89] Eruvin 100b; Avos Drab Nassan Ch. 1; Tractate Yevamos 62b

[90] See Gen. 3:16-19 and see Bereshit Raba 20:10

within it. As the body undergoes this process, the woman becomes unholy, which is what *niddah* is. It's important to add that although this is an unholy state, it is not a sin to remain in this condition. Technically, a woman can stay in a state of *tummah*, impurity, her whole life.

A deeper, and perhaps more relatable reason for menstruation is to create a greater bond and passion between husband and wife that emerges from separation. However, this doesn't explain why the woman was the one chosen to become *niddah*. The Kabbalistic answer is that because a woman comes from a higher level of purity, she is thereby more sensitive to impurity. As the Talmud says, *binah yiseira nitna l'esha*[91] "a greater level of understanding, or sensitivity, was given to the woman." Furthermore, King Solomon says *aishes chayil ateres balah*[92]: "the woman of valor is the crown of her husband." Simply put, a woman's understanding of these things transcends that of her husband. She is one who is compared to the holy land of Israel; therefore, she's the one that needs to expel this impurity from her body.[93]

Rabbi Moshe Tendler once said that the Lubavitcher Rebbe told him, "Many people think that when you're dealing with a couple who is coming closer to *Yiddishkeit*, to Judaism, you should first talk about other mitzvot, kosher and charity, and things like that. Later, when you see they are really, really committed, then you go into the whole concept of *mikvah* and family purity." The Rebbe, however, believed the opposite to be true. "First talk about *mikvah*."

Rabbi Tendler explained this position as he understood it to be: "Today, we find so many problems with relationships, in that people simply can't get a handle on them. How do we communicate with each other? How do we continue to experience this passion in our marriage? As the Rebbe correctly said, "the first thing you have to talk about is *mikvah*, because this is all about the foundation of relationships and bringing passion back into your marriage."

---

[91] Niddah 45b. Breishis Rabba 18:1
[92] Proverbs 31:10
[93] in Hebrew land is translated as *eretz* which in kabbalah is the attribute malchus which is feminine.

The mitzvah of *mikvah* has many, many benefits and positive side effects. The first positive side effect is that it truly brings passion back into the marriage.

I once met with a lawyer in downtown Brooklyn, who told me he had a girlfriend in Florida. Every six months he would go visit her and it was all fireworks. As he was trying to make me jealous, I needed to answer him with something great.

After he finished his spiel, I said to him, "I really feel sorry for you, because you are so deprived. You have to wait six months to have fireworks in your relationship. I have fireworks every single month."

In truth, every home that observes the laws of *mikvah* experiences fireworks every month when the wife comes home from the *mikvah* until she gets her next period.

Every mitzvah has tangible, positive side effects. The *mikvah*, in addition to fulfilling G-d's command and bringing passion back into marriage, also provides blessing for producing healthy and productive children. As the Rebbe assured, "Going to mikvah is a good omen to conceive children and give birth to healthy beautiful children, who will live a long and productive life."[94]

Despite the positive aspects of *mikvah*, there are a lot of negative connotations surrounding this beautiful mitzvah. Many confuse the word "impure" with "dirty" and think that separating a woman from her husband is done for belittling reasons.

To that end, I was once confronted by a young woman wielding a steady barrage of questions. "Why are women impure? Why do women have to go to the *mikvah*? Why aren't men impure? Why is the Torah so male chauvinistic?"

I understood that her questions stemmed from a fundamental misunderstanding of what this mitzvah is about. The only way to quell the anger would be with a full explanation that went back to the beginning.

---

[94] Lubavitcher Rebbe's talk 12 Tamuz 5724.

I explained that it's true that married women go to *mikvah* once a month, twelve days after their period; however, Chassidic men go to *mikvah* every morning before their daily prayer.[95] Technically, men go thirty times a month instead of only once. Secondly, only someone who is holy can become unholy or impure. It is also important to note that the idea of *tumma*, which we translate to mean "impure," etymologically comes from the word that means blockage. In other words, if a doorway is blocked, you cannot enter. Similarly when a woman becomes *niddah*, when she menstruates, according to Torah law she assumes a state of *tumma*. There is a spiritual blockage, and the husband is not allowed to enter. Now, it is in no way a sin to be in a state of *tumma*. A woman could be in that state of *tumma* all of her life, but if the husband wants to enter, then the wife is required to immerse in a *mikvah*.

Furthermore, as stated above, the concept of *tumma*, or impurity, primarily applies to Jews. As the Torah states, "You shall be for me a nation of priests and a holy people."[96] This is because only something that is intrinsically holy can become unholy and impure. Something which is not holy to begin with cannot become *tammay*, cannot become impure. This also connects to why the Kabbalah says that the powers of *k'lipa*, the powers of unholiness, are nourished through holiness.[97] They siphon it to acquire vitality because true life can only come from holiness. As the Torah says, "And you cleave in the L-rd your G-D... You are therefore all alive today."[98] True life is holiness, cleaving unto G-d. However, holiness is too bright and overwhelming, so the *k'lipa* can only attach itself when that light is dimmed. When one becomes *tammay*, the energy is blocked and diminished, so the powers of impurity can latch on and that's when one becomes impure.

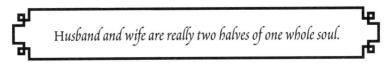

Husband and wife are really two halves of one whole soul.

The great mystic and Kabbalist, the AriZal, taught that a husband and wife are really two halves of one whole soul.[99] When a woman is

---

95 Likkutei Torah Tavo 43b-c.

96 Exodus 19:6

97 See Tanya Chapter 6; Rambam Laws of Tumas meis chap.1 law 13.

98 Deuteronomy 4:4

99 Zohar Vol. III page 7b; Toras Menachem Acharon Shel Pesach 5730.

niddah, the man is also spiritually *niddah,* so it's not just the wife who must separate from her husband, but the husband must also separate from his wife. Thereby, when the husband encourages his wife to go to *mikvah,* and celebrates this holy mitzvah, the husband also becomes a participant. A similar situation occurs when a husband puts on tefillin. The wife receives credit for putting on tefillin because she is half the soul of the husband and supports his doing this mitzvah. So, in truth, *mikvah* is really a joint mitzvah, made possible through a partnership of the husband and wife supporting each other.

Another misconception about mikvah was evident in the reaction of a woman I met a few years ago. The young woman had been pregnant with twins, but sadly lost one of her babies at birth. Despite the joy of having a newborn, she was broken over the loss of the other baby. To help her find closure, I suggested she use the *mikvah.*

"Ew, I would never do that!" she exclaimed. "My mother told me that it's dirty and there are things swimming around in there."

Rather than argue further, I took her on a tour of our *mikvah,* an action which spoke louder than any words. The woman had the same reaction that Oprah did when she saw our synagogue's mikvah. "This is like a spa! It's amazing, it's gorgeous!"

> *The woman had the same reaction that Oprah did when she saw our synagogue's mikvah. "This is like a spa! It's amazing, it's gorgeous!"*

This is the way a *mikvah* is supposed to be. Like other mitzvot, a *mikvah* should be enticing, inviting and built in the most beautiful way possible.

Many people mistakenly believe that the mitzvah of *mikvah* originates from times when there was no indoor plumbing and people went to public bathhouses to bathe. These individuals believe that after a woman menstruated she went to a public bath, the modern equivalent would be immersing in a *mikvah,* to clean herself after her impurity.

This idea is sorely misguided and missing the truth. According to Jewish law, *Halacha,* the laws of *mikvah* were passed down from Moses at Mt. Sinai and have nothing to do with modern day conveniences, or past inconveniences. Rather, *Halacha* states that a woman must physically cleanse herself *before* she uses the *mikvah*.[100] Most women soak in a bath from twenty minutes to half an hour, just to be certain that they are absolutely clean. Then they make sure there are no foreign objects, for example nail polish must be removed, that can separate them from the purifying waters of the *mikvah*.

This care and preparation shows that the waters of the *mikvah* are really a spiritual transformation, not just a physical transformation.[101] According to Jewish law and mysticism, the mikvah needs to have forty *seah*, a Talmudic measurement (equal to about 160-200 gallons of water). The number forty represents transformation. For example, the flood that G-d brought upon the world during the time of Noah lasted 40 days and nights in order to purify the world like a *mikvah*.[102]

Menopause

The mitzvah of *mikvah* is not only relevant for younger women, who are capable of having children and still menstruate, but also for women who have reached, or passed, menopause. A woman who hasn't gone to *mikvah* after her last period can and is encouraged to immerse in the *mikvah*, if she is still married.[103] Not only will she now be in a permanent state of holiness and purity, but going to the *mikvah* with the proper intent could retroactively fix all the times she missed out until now.

A young girl was suffering from severe emotional issues, so her mother wrote a letter to the Rebbe requesting a blessing for her emotional health. The Rebbe asked his secretaries to find out whether or not the mother kept the laws of *mikvah* and if the daughter was born in purity. The Rebbe's question implied that this could be the reason for her instability, and that the mother could retroactively correct it by going to the *mikvah*.

---

[100] Code of the Jewish Law Yoreh Deah Ch. 198.

[101] See Rambam Laws of Mikvah, at the end.

[102] Torah Ohr, Noach Page 16a.

[103] Sichos Kodesh Rosh Chodesh Elul 5735, Ch. 4

MIKVAH preparation Checklist

12 Days after one's period, one prepares to enter into the Mikvah in the following way:

- Remove make-up and skin lotions.
- Remove nail polish. Cut, file and clean finger and toe nails.
- Brush teeth; no particles of food should remain between teeth. Use dental floss (unwaxed preferred), only if you are sure it will not get caught between teeth. Rinse mouth with water.
- Bathe with warm water. Wash entire body thoroughly. Use soap and washcloth or loofah sponge
- Smooth hard skin and calluses. Soften and remove dry scabs provided bleeding will not occur.
- Remove protruding splinters.
- Wash hair with shampoo, without conditioners.*
- Shower or rinse thoroughly with a non-moisturizing soap or body wash.
- Comb all hair while still wet. It is helpful to place a towel under the hair so loose hair will not fall on body.
- If preparations are made at home, shower and re-comb your hair at the mikvah.

- Check your body, using a mirror when needed to ensure that you are free of intervening substances.
- Signal to the Mikvah attendant that you are ready.
- The mikvah attendant will assist you in the mikvah room and remain present during your immersion to pronounce it kosher upon completion.

When you are in the water recite the following Blessing:

Ba-ruch a-toh A-doh-noi E-lo-hai-nu me-lech ho-o-lom a-sher ki-d'-sho-nu b'-mitz-vo-sov vitzi-vo-nu al ha-t'-vi-loh.

Translation: Blessed are you, L-rd our G-d, King of the universe, who has sanctified us with His commandments, and commanded us on the immersion.

(For more info see www.mikvah.org)

On one occasion, the Rebbe mentioned that many holy books wonder why there is a "degeneration in our generation,"[104] meaning, why has our generation fallen from the spiritual heights of the generations living in Europe and well before that? A conclusion of many leading rabbis is that this results from the lack of *mikvah* observance. When a woman becomes pregnant after using the *mikvah*, her child is born with its soul wrapped in a holy *levush*, a garment that inspires, protects and warms the soul to spirituality.[105] Children born outside of this observance lack that holy garment and are therefore more susceptible to the impurities and toxins of the surrounding world.

A woman once wrote a letter to the Rebbe, in which she expressed how upset she was that her Jewish son was living with a non-Jewish woman. Theologically and philosophically, marriage between a Jew and non-Jew is not allowed and could be very counterproductive for both sides. Here too, the Rebbe asked if the child was born in purity, and if not, it was not too late for the mother to rectify this. Luckily, *mikvah* is a mitzvah that can retroactively repair the damage, because the spiritual world is not bound by time or space.

In short, how can someone make things "right?"

1. Start going to *mikvah* now.

2. Try to influence at least two other women to go to *mikvah* as well.

3. Increase in giving charity, not necessarily by giving large amounts, but rather in the frequency of giving. Keep a charity box in your kitchen and put a few coins in every day. Maimonides teaches that a mitzvah is performed each time you put a coin into a charity box, so the more times you give the more mitzvot you do.[106] This mitzvah is significant because charity brings atonement and redemption, a fitting action to do before going into the *mikvah*.

The prophet Ezekiel, referring to The Messianic Era, states in the name of G-d, "Then I will sprinkle the pure waters upon you, and you

---

[104] Likkutei Sichos Vol. 13 page 259.
[105] See Tanya Ch. 2 in the name of the AriZal.
[106] See Rambam's commentary on Avos 3:15.

will truly be purified."[107] Keeping the laws of mikvah and following all of these precepts will no doubt hasten the coming of the Moshiach. This will usher in a time when G-d will bring the whole world to a level of purity, and will erase all that is abnormal, toxic and non-kosher, bringing peace, harmony and purity, not only between husband and wife, but between G-d and His people and all the nations of the world.

Story

A congregant once told me about his grandparents who arrived in Bismarck, North Dakota in 1905, a place that attracted many German immigrants. They had four daughters, all of whom had little interest in Judaism. One daughter, Beatrice, even became an atheist as a defense mechanism to avoid getting caught up in politics because of her religion. After some time, the family moved to Minnesota where Beatrice married and gave birth to a daughter. Her daughter Esther encountered Chabad in Minnesota, and eventually attended the Bais Chana School for girls where she met Rabbi Manis Friedman, who became her teacher and mentor. With time, Esther became religious and ended up marrying a follower of Chabad teachings. Esther was married for a number of years, but was unfortunately unable to bear any children. She went to the *mikvah* monthly as she was supposed to, and studied the laws carefully to make sure she did everything right. She even went to doctors and tried in vitro fertilization and other such procedures to no avail.

Finally, she wrote a letter to the Lubavitcher Rebbe about her situation and asked for a blessing. A few days later she received a telephone call from Rabbi Laibel Groner, one of the Rebbe's secretaries. "The Rebbe suggested that you ask your mother to go to *mikvah*."

Esther asked Beatrice if she would be willing to go, but being as she was an atheist, she refused. Esther wrote back to the Rebbe telling of her mother's refusal and soon received another phone call from Rabbi Groner. "The Rebbe suggests that you ask your grandmother to go to *mikvah*."

Esther called up her grandmother and asked her if she would be willing to go the *mikvah* so she would be blessed with a child.

---
[107] Ezekiel 36:25

Esther's grandmother asked her husband what he thought of the prospect and his response was immediate, "What wouldn't a grandparent do for a grandchild? Of course you should go."

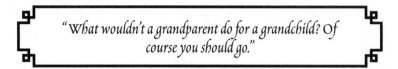

"What wouldn't a grandparent do for a grandchild? Of course you should go."

The grandmother went to the *mikvah*, and a month later Esther became pregnant with the first of her *nine* children.

This story clearly shows that the mitzvah of *mikvah* is not only a personal mitzvah, but also one that affects your children for generations to come. It also proves that it is never too late to start, and even if you're at a point where you only need to go once, retroactively you can still impact many generations to come.

CHAPTER 6

Mechitzah: Should We Separate Men and Women During Prayer?

John Gray has said that men are from Mars and women are from Venus. According to Kabbalah, men are from Chochmah, and women are from Binah.[108] *Chochmah,* or wisdom, is the first attribute of the intellectual faculty, the *concept* of a seminal idea. *Binah,* or understanding, is the second attribute of the intellectual faculty, the period of gestation that develops the seminal drop and elaborates upon it. The Zohar states that these two faculties of *Chochmah* and *Binah* are, "Two friends that never separate." In other words, they need and complement each other. *Chochmah* without *Binah* is simply a pie in the sky. *Binah* without *Chochmah* is a fuss over nothing.

> *John Gray has said that men are from Mars and women are from Venus. According to Kabbalah, men are from Chochmah, and women are from Binah.*

So, if men and women are both so alike and dependent on each other, why is it that in the synagogue men and women are separated by a *mechitzah*, particularly during prayer?

---

[108] See Tanya Ch. 3.

An interesting note to consider along these lines is that the layout of modern synagogues is very similar to the *Beit HaMikdash*, the Holy Temple which stood in Jerusalem, also considered to be the first synagogue. The blueprints of that original synagogue were drawn up by G-d Himself and given to King David, whose son King Solomon built it. In the *Beit HaMikdash* women and men were separated.[109]

I believe the answer to this seemingly contradictory practice is found in Jewish law where it states that during intimacy, a man is not allowed to think about another woman.[110] That's an actual law. Seeing a law like this may lead one to wonder, *What about other times?* Is a man permitted to think of being intimate with other women at times when he is not being intimate with his wife? No, he is not! So why does the law specify "during intimacy"? The simple answer is that this law was written at a time when polygamy was allowed and so a man was permitted to have more than one wife. For example, Jacob, our forefather had two wives, Rachel and Leah. Therefore, when Jacob was with Leah, even though Leah was his second wife, he wasn't allowed to be thinking about Rachel; he must be with Leah physically, emotionally and spiritually. This concept also applies to the synagogue.

When considering what prayer is all about, our Rabbis say "*da lifnei mi attah omed* - know before whom you stand."[111] The word *da*, from the word *da'at*, doesn't only mean to know, but is also a euphemism for intimacy. The first use of *da'at* in this way is found in Genesis: "And Adam knew his wife Eve, and he begat children."[112] Knowing your wife long distance will not beget children, so it is understood that here the Torah uses the word *da'at*, knowledge or to know, as a euphemism for intimacy.

Chassidic philosophy teaches that there are three levels to wisdom (remember two were referenced above), or three parts of the brain:

1. *Chochmah*, translated as wisdom, refers to the initial conception of an idea, that first flash of intellect like a lightning bolt.

---

109 Igrot Kodesh, Vol. 7, P. 309, see there references in Rambam and other halachic sources pertaining to mechitzah.

110 Rambam, Issurei Biah, Ch.21, Law 12.

111 English letter of the Rebbe on Mechitzah, 10 Nissan 5721 (found on Chabad.org under mechitzah), see similar letter in Igrot Kodesh, Vol. 18, P. 394-5.

112 Genesis 4:1

2. *Binah,* translated as understanding, is the exposition of that initial flash until it takes form and becomes an actual idea or concept.

3. *Da'at,* translated as knowledge, is the ability to take an idea and bring it into actual action or application.

The connection between *da'at* and prayer stems from the fundamental objective of prayer, which is that man and G-d become one. Prayer is, therefore, the intimate setting during which an individual is forbidden to think about anyone else, so we use a *mechitzah* to separate men from women.

Imagine a man sitting in prayer, and tells G-d, *V'ahavta,* "I love you with all my heart, with all my soul, with all my might." How does G-d respond? "Really? So who's that beautiful woman sitting next to you? You can't tell Me you're only thinking about Me; you're also thinking about her." And vice-versa. If a woman says, "G-d, I love you with all my heart and with all my soul, with all my might," while sitting next to a handsome young fellow, G-d says, "Really? Are you thinking about Me or are you thinking about him? Remember, I know your inner thoughts.". Therefore, to eliminate distraction and truly focus on having an intimate relationship with G-d, we need to separate the sexes because they distract each other.

The *mechitzah* is not only necessary to eliminate distraction, but also to eliminate conversation, another aspect in this example of intimacy. Can you imagine, if at a time of intimacy with your partner and spouse, all of a sudden your cell phone goes off and you tell your partner, "Hold on, I've got to take this call?"

> *Can you imagine, if at a time of intimacy with your partner and spouse, all of a sudden your cell phone goes off and you tell your partner, "Hold on, I've got to take this call?*

Your partner is going to throw you out of the bedroom. "That phone call is more important than me? You just told me how much you love me. You just told me that I am the apple of your eye. You just told me that there's nothing in the world that matters besides me, and all of a sudden you're taking that call?"

Prayer is our time of intimacy with G-d, and when you start talking to your neighbor G-d says, "Hello, are you taking that call? Is that mortal more important than me? Did it ever occur to you that you are having intimacy with Me, or is that person sitting next to you more important than our relationship?"

In Tanya, the Alter Rebbe explains that during prayer we stand face-to-face with G-d, the King of all kings, in His private chamber.[113] Imagine all of a sudden you tell G-d, "King, please excuse me a moment, I've got to take this call." Can you imagine the gravity of that sin? That would be considered rebelling against the king and earn the perpetrator a beheading on the spot! This is the seriousness of prayer. It is to know you are standing before G-d, the King of all kings. How can you converse with someone else? Just as it is wrong for a man to talk to a woman during prayer, it is equally prohibited for a man to talk to his friend or a woman to talk to her friend during prayer. This is one reason why men wear a tallit (or prayer shawl) during prayer over their heads. With it they create a blinder and a *mechitzah*, to separate between one man and his neighbor.

Theoretically, a synagogue should be made up of enclosed cubicles so that every individual can separate themselves and give full attention to their intimate time with G-d. So not only should there be a separation between men and women during prayer, but really, there should be a *mechitzah* between man and man or woman and woman. The best reason I've come up with as to why we cannot do this is because this would be a fire hazard, so instead, we try to set basic parameters. We eliminate the basic distractions by keeping men on one side and women on the other side. Then both the men and women will practice not speaking to their neighbors.

There's another law that supports the idea that prayer is a time of intimacy with G-d. In the Code of Jewish Law it states that a father or a mother may not kiss their child while standing in a synagogue because a synagogue is a place of romance between man and G-d.[114] Even though the love of a parent for a child is applauded, and it's even a love that we beseech G-d to emulate "just like a father has mercy on his children,

---

[113] Igeres Hakodesh, Ch. 24
[114] Alter Rebbe's Shulchan Aruch, Ch. 98:1

G-d, YOU have mercy upon us."[115] Yet, in the synagogue, our love is dedicated to one place and focused on one reality—G-d.

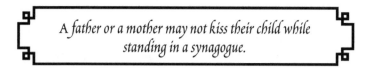

A father or a mother may not kiss their child while standing in a synagogue.

Story

Rabbi Aaron of Belz arrived at the gates of Haifa, on the 9th of Shvat, 1944. When he entered into a local synagogue to pray, he noticed that there was no section for woman to pray. He refused to pray the services in that place.

His Chassidim asked him, "Rebbe, is it not true that one does not need women for the minyan? Could we not daven without the women's section?"

The Belzer Rav responded, "Since the Temple was destroyed, the gates for prayer have closed, but the gates for tears have never closed. When woman pray, they pray with tears. We need the women to pray together with us in our synagogue."

---

[115] Psalms, Ch. 113:13

CHAPTER 7

Do Women Count?

"Okay, Rabbi," I hear you saying, "I agree a *mechitzah* makes sense to eliminate distraction in the synagogue, but now I've got another question. Why can't we count women for the *minyan*? If we have five men on one side of the *mechitzah* and five women on the other side, then we have a *minyan,* a quorum of ten people. Why does it matter whether it's men, or women that make up that number?"

The most common answer given for this question comes from the tradition that a *minyan* became necessary because of the sin of the spies in the desert. We read in the book of Numbers that Moses chose twelve spies to scout the Land of Israel and help devise a plan of how best to conquer it. Ten of the spies returned with a negative report claiming the land consumes its inhabitants, and that even G-d cannot conquer it.[116] This report caused the Jewish nation to lose faith in G-d's promise to bring them into the Holy Land and created doubt in His omnipotence. G-d thereafter punished the Jewish people by making them wander in the desert for forty years, declaring "How much longer must I deal with this evil congregation?"[117]

The Talmud derives from this statement that a *minyan* is made up of ten men, as the ten spies who brought about this wandering were men

---

116   Numbers 13-14
117   Numbers 14:27

not women.[118] G-d's rhetorical question in response to the incident also indicates that it takes ten men to establish a "congregation." Since then, men pray with a *minyan* to atone for the sin of the spies.

However, I believe there is a deeper, more complimentary answer as to why women are not counted in a *minyan*. The concept of counting is associated with limitation and death, which we find in the Torah when G-d tells Moses to count the men from the ages of twenty to sixty, each of whom must give half a shekel as atonement for their soul.[119] It is specifically the *men* who must give because they are atoning for the sin of the golden calf. As mentioned previously, the women didn't need to seek atonement because they did not participate in this sin and so were not counted by Moses. Also, the men who were counted would not be allowed to enter the Holy Land and were destined to die over the next forty years in the desert.

As a side note, G-d instructed Moses to count the tribe of Levi, who also did not sin by worshipping the golden calf, separately from the other men. Additionally, the Levites were counted from thirty days and older[120]. Rashi says that as the Levites served G-d in the Tabernacle in the desert, and would eventually serve Him in the *Beit HaMikdash*, it was fitting that the legion of the king be counted separately. Like the women, the men from the tribe of Levi did not die over the next forty years in the desert.

However, these proofs further strengthen the question of why women aren't counted. The answer is found in the life of Moses' brother, Aaron the High Priest. Aaron was the one who was supposed to help Moses count the tribe of Levi, and we are told according to the opinion of Rashi that Aaron was not counted with his tribe.[121] Why not? Aaron was of the tribe of Levi, so why wasn't he counted?

The Lubavitcher Rebbe says the reason that Aaron the High Priest was not counted is simply because Aaron was so attached to G-d that he was beyond number.[122] In other words, he wore more than one hat

---

118 Tractate Sanhedrin, Ch. 1, Mishna 6
119 Exodus Tisa 30:12
120 Ibid, 3:15
121 Numbers 3:39. See Rashi's commentary.
122 Likkutei Sichos Vol. 33 P. 8

and was not limited to one job. He was Moses confidant, he was Moses interpreter before Pharaoh, he was the High Priest, the holiest Jew, who entered the holiest place on earth, the holy of holies in the holy temple on the holiest day of the year, known as Yom Kippur or the Day of Atonement. He brought the sacrifices of the Jewish people before G-d, he brought the Jews closer to G-d and he was also the first official marriage counselor.[123] If he knew of a husband who left his wife, he might tell him, "You know, your wife loves you. She can't sleep at night. She wants you home." Because of this, the husband's love for his wife would be reawakened and he would return home. At the same time Aaron would tell the wife, "Your husband cannot live without you. Please let him back into the house." Aaron was also the official outreach director. Any Jew that left the camp, Aaron would go outside of the Clouds of Glory and bring him back in. With Aaron having so many responsibilities, the Torah says he can't be counted only as one. Elijah the Prophet gives G-d the same compliment when he proclaims, "You are one and unique, but you cannot be counted because you're beyond number."[124]

Women who have the ability to emulate G-d by bringing children into the world and wear multiple hats on any given day are truly unique and beyond number. A woman is her husband's confidante, the mother of their children, the family psychiatrist, the family doctor, interior decorator, educational director, chef and so on.

(By the way, the main job of the *Kohanim* or Priests in the Holy Temple was to be the chefs and bakers. They used to slaughter the animals, fillet the meat then burn some of it on the altar, and cook some for human consumption. They also baked the showbreads weekly. This was considered the greatest service among the people of Israel).

Women have so many responsibilities, they emulate G-d more than men in this regard, and are not counted; they are one and unique and truly beyond the limitations of numbers.

---

123 Avos Drebbi, Noson Ch. 12
124 Tikunei Zohar, Introduction, p. 13A. Also in the Kehot Siddur, P. 125.

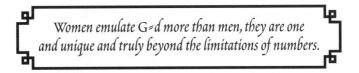

Women emulate G-d more than men, they are one and unique and truly beyond the limitations of numbers.

Story

A rabbi in California once called Lubavitch World Headquarters, located at 770 Eastern Parkway, Brooklyn, with a pressing question. Rabbi Chaim Mordechai Isaac Hodakov, the Rebbe's Chief of the Secretariat, answered the phone.

"What should we do?" the rabbi asked. "There are women here who want to start a woman's prayer group. We checked it out according to Halacha and it seems to be okay. Is it something that we should support or not?"

"Give me some time, I need to look into it," Rabbi Hodakov responded. (We don't know if his response came from the Rebbe directly or indirectly, but this was Rabbi Hodakov's response).

Soon after, Rabbi Hodakov came back with the following answer. "Our Rabbis tell us that a synagogue is considered to be a miniature replica of the Beit Hamikdash, the holy temple that stood in Jerusalem;[125] therefore, what was in the Temple must be in the synagogue. Just like in the Holy Temple men and women prayed simultaneously but separated side-by-side, the same should be done in our miniature Temples, aka the synagogue."

---

[125] Talmud Megilla

CHAPTER 8

Should Women Wear Tallit and Tefillin?

I trust we have found an agreement on *mechitzah* and *minyan*, and women still need to pray. As Maimonides says in regard to prayer, "If you need something, ask for it."[126] I believe that, at the very least, we can agree that we all need G-d's blessings and intervention on a daily basis. So, as a woman wants to pray like a man does, can she wear *a tallit* or *tefillin* to enhance her meditation in prayer?

As we discussed, there are 613 commandments in the Torah, 248 positive ones and 365 negative ones. Among these commandments are those that are restricted to a specific time and place, which women are often exempt from. However, there are six mitzvot, which transcend every time and place, as they are twenty-four hours a day, seven days a week, without exception.[127] They are:

1. Belief in G-d.

2. Not to believe in other gods.

3. To believe in the Oneness of G-d, that G-d permeates every aspect of reality.

4. To love G-d.

---

126   Derech Mitzvosecho (Of the Tzemech Tzedek) mitzvah of Teffilah.
127   Introduction to the Sefer Hachinuch.

5. To have awe and respect for G-d.

6. To not follow our heart's desire and what our eyes see.

The Talmud rules that women are not obligated to observe any positive commandment restricted to a specific time.[128] As these six commandments aren't, women are obligated to observe them, perhaps even more than men, who are busy fulfilling mitzvot that are time-bound. Therefore, the primary burden of responsibility for these mitzvot falls on the women.

A great Chassidic leader came to visit the Lubavitcher Rebbe to ask, "Is it true that in your Chabad Lubavitch schools, girls are taught Chassidic philosophy (which reveals the secrets and the mystical aspects of the Torah)? How is it that you teach girls these esoteric teachings?"

The Rebbe responded, "On the contrary, women also need to learn Chassidus and perhaps even more than men because they need to follow these six mitzvot twenty-four hours a day. The only way one can truly believe in G-d, know G-d and understand His oneness is through the study of Chassidus. The teachings of Chassidus primarily focus on the unity of G-d and the infinity of G-d, so therefore, we teach the girls Chassidus."[129]

Continuing with the idea that women are not obligated in time-bound mitzvot, *tefillin* and *tzitzit* are two examples of mitzvot that are restricted to a specific time and place. In reference to *tzitzit*, the Torah states, "You shall *see them* and remind yourself of all the commandments."[130] The commentators explain this verse implies that *tzitzit* should be worn when you can see them, as in during the day. In modern times, with the convenience of electricity, *tzitzit* can be seen at all hours of the day, but the implication here is natural daylight. Therefore, this mitzvah would be considered a time restricted one, and women are exempt from its fulfillment. *Tefillin,* which are worn during the week but not on Shabbat, are also bound by a specific time and so women are exempt from wearing them.

---

[128] Talmud Kiddushin 35.
[129] Toras Menachem 5741, Vol. 2 P. 810.
[130] Numbers 15:39

Even though women are exempt from *tefillin* and *tzitzit*, does that mean a woman who wants to wear them cannot? Some codifiers say that women should not and are even forbidden to wear them[131] because of the basic Torah law that "a man shall not wear the garments of a woman, and similarly, a woman shall not wear the garments of a man."[132] According to this opinion, *tzitzit* and *tefillin* are masculine garments; therefore, a female should not wear them.

However, this is not the halachic ruling. On the contrary, and quite surprisingly, the Alter Rebbe writes pertaining to the mitzvah of *tzitzit* that a woman can wear them if she wants, and even make the *bracha*, "That you have commanded me with this mitzvah of putting on *tzitzis*."[133] However, he concludes that she should not because it is *mechzei k'urah*; it makes a person seem conceited or arrogant. The reason for this is, in essence, the mitzvah of *tzitzit*, even for a man, is not an obligation on the body, but an obligation on the article. Meaning, if a man wears a four-cornered garment, he has an obligation to put the *tzitzit*, strings on the corners. If a woman puts on *tzitzit*, not only is she doing a mitzvah that she's not obligated to do, but she's doing a mitzvah that even a man is not obligated to do (unless he wears a four-cornered garment). As there are so many more important mitzvot to do, why should she choose this mitzvah over the others? If a woman truly, truly wants to, however, the Alter Rebbe says she's allowed to do so.

This decision contrasts sharply with *tefillin*, which the Alter Rebbe says a woman should not do.[134] Halacha rules that women should be dissuaded from putting them on, and even goes so far as to protest if a woman puts on *tefillin*. Why? What's the big deal?

I saw a very interesting interpretation in the *Hagaos Maimones*, a commentary on Maimonides, which teaches that when it comes to *tefillin*, there is a basic problem with modesty.[135] *Tefillin* are wrapped around the arm, all the way above the elbow on the bicep, but a woman is supposed to keep her arms covered below her elbow. For a woman to

---

131 See Targum Yonasan Ben Uziel - Deuteronomy 22:5
132 Deuteronomy 22:5
133 Code Of the Jewish Law, Ch. 17
134 Code Of the Jewish Law 38:3
135 Laws of Tzitzis, Ch. 3, note 30

put on *tefillin*, she'd have to roll up her sleeve in public and expose her arm above her elbow, which is not in line with the laws of modesty. Along this same reasoning, according to *Halacha,* a married woman must cover her hair. She can wear a *sheitel* (a wig) or a hat, but either way she must keep her hair covered. In this case, how can she wear *tefillin* for the head? Will she take off her hat or *sheitel,* or will she push it back so her hair is exposed? Halacha refers to a married woman's uncovered hair as actual nakedness[136] so she can hardly be allowed to reveal her hair just so she can put on *tefillin*. However, just to note, the Alter Rebbe does not state this answer in his Code of Jewish Law.

I believe the reason why women don't put on *tefillin* is connected to the law that we do not put on *tefillin* on Shabbat. Shabbat is feminine. This point is supported in the Friday Night prayer of *L'chah Dodi,* in which we sing: "Let us go my beloved toward the bride, the countenance of Shabbat,"[137] wherein Shabbat is the bride. A woman is the manifestation of Shabbat every single day of the week. The man does not don *tefillin* on Shabbat, and if he did we would protest. So too a woman, who is the embodiment of Shabbat, does not put on *tefillin*. This is also true Kabbalistically. Women are generally associated with the feminine attribute of *malchut* or kingship,[138] the name for the seventh supernal *sefirot* or attributes, which is the same attribute as Shabbat.

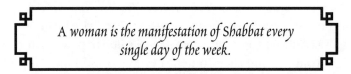

A *woman is the manifestation of Shabbat every single day of the week.*

A woman may be adamant about putting on *tefillin* but our response to this is similar to the ruling about sounding the shofar when Rosh Hashana falls out on Shabbat. Sounding the shofar on Rosh Hashana, the Jewish New Year, brings a new light and energy into this world for the year ahead. However, if Rosh Hashana comes out on Shabbat, the shofar

---

136 Talmud Brachos 24a. Code of the Jewish Law Ch. 75
137 Prayer of Kabolas Shabbat.
138 Even though we stated earlier, women represent the attribute of *bina* or understanding, that is true of the intellectual faculties. However, on the level of the *middot* or emotions, they represent *malchut* or kingship.

is not sounded because Shabbat itself brings down that light and energy.[139] *Tefillin* are not worn on Shabbat for similar reasons. The new energy that we bring into each day by wearing *tefillin* is achieved through the holiness of Shabbat. Essentially, putting on *tefillin* on Shabbat is redundant and doesn't count as any sort of accomplishment; whatever someone would achieve is already there and cannot be increased by wearing *tefillin*. In addition to Shabbat, *tefillin* are not worn on major holidays like Passover and Sukkot, including their intermediate weekdays.

Halacha states that men do not put on *tefillin* on Shabbat because *teffilin* are a sign,[140] as it states in the Torah, "Tefillin shall be for you a *sign* on your hand… and between your eyes."[141] Shabbat is also a sign, as it's written, "Keep my Shabbat for is it a *sign* between me and you… That you may know that I am the L-rd who sanctifies you" (L-rd added).[142] Once we have one sign, we don't need another one. Woman are Shabbat, women are that sign, so wearing *tefillin* would merely be a redundancy.

Taking another approach, the explanation can also be applied to a seemingly uncomplimentary statement about women in the Talmud that states the *da'at* of women is *kalut*.[143] The simple and often used translation of *kalut* is the word "weak," which would mean that the Talmud seems to imply that women's knowledge is weak, though we know this isn't the case. Not only are many women smarter than men, but girls celebrate their Bat Mitzvah at the age of twelve because they mature faster than boys. The Talmud contradicts its own assertion by declaring that a greater level of understanding was given to the woman over the man.[144]

> Not only are many women smarter than men, but girls celebrate their Bat Mitzvah at the age of twelve because they mature faster than boys.

---

[139] Likkutei Torah Rosh Hashana 57a.
[140] Or major holidays like the 8 days of Passover and 9 days of Succot and Simchat Torah :see story at end of chapter.
[141] Exodus 13:9
[142] Exodus 31:13
[143] Tractate Shabbat 33b
[144] Tractate Niddah 45b

The simple interpretations of these phrases (i.e. that women are more emotional than men) are not enough, but through the eyes of Chassidus we can understand it in a new light. As explained before, *bina* means understanding and *da'at* means applying knowledge to action. Therefore, when the Talmud says that a woman's *da'at* is *kalut*, what it really means is that it is *kal,* **easy**[145] (not weak), for women in general to apply their understanding to action.

An example of this is when a man goes to a Torah class. When he comes home, his wife asks him, "So, what did you learn?"

"Oh, the Rabbi spoke about kosher."

"Really? Are we going to start keeping kosher?" the wife asks.

"We'll worry about it tomorrow." He shrugs it off, goes to sleep and forgets about it.

When a woman comes home from that same Torah class, she begins to throw away all of her non-kosher food and dishes into the garbage and is already online ordering two new sets of dishes for milk and meat, even before her husband says, "What's going on over here?"

"The Rabbi spoke about keeping kosher tonight," she explains, "so I'm making it happen."

That is an example of easily applying wisdom and understanding into action, which connects back to the reason why women don't wear *tefillin*. Men put *Tefillin* on their heads with straps draping down the side, to the navel[146] and even beyond that, symbolizing the idea of taking knowledge and bringing it from the head to the lower parts of the body, bringing it into action. Women don't need to put on *tefillin* to accomplish this; it comes naturally.

Story

The Zohar relates the following parable of a king, who told his dedicated servant to have a copy made of his royal signet ring so that

---

145 See Likkutei Torah, Chukas, pg. 60d.
146 Code of the Jewish Law of the Alter Rebbe Ch. 27 Law 20.

the servant would always be protected from harm. Later on, the king's admiration for his servant grew and the king gave him his own personal ring. "Now can you imagine," asks the Zohar, "if the servant would remove the king's personal ring in favor of his old copy of the ring? Surely it would be considered an affront to the king, possibly one the servant would have to pay for with his life!"

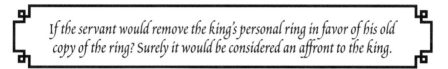

If the servant would remove the king's personal ring in favor of his old copy of the ring? Surely it would be considered an affront to the king.

"The same is true for these holidays," the Zohar explains, "when G-d gives us his personal *tefillin* to wear. How dare we remove His in favor of our own?"

CHAPTER 9

Women Scholars and Torah Study

The Midrash teaches, "A kosher woman creates the will of her husband."[147] That is to say, she has the power to inspire her husband and her entire family. With this we introduce the next concept: Torah study. Men have an obligation to study Torah day and night, but women do not. Unfortunately, this has often led to times when women were not taught or encouraged to study Torah at all; if they were taught anything, it was simplified concepts or only stories and not actual laws. The Alter Rebbe writes in the Code of Jewish Law that a woman should make a blessing before learning Torah just like men.[148] This seems to indicate that women are encouraged to learn Torah, especially so they know how to apply their three mitzvot in actual practice. Also, a woman who studies Torah receives reward for her Torah study.

It's been said in the name of the Chofetz Chaim that if a man would only be fluent in the laws applicable to women, then he would truly be a Torah giant, because women need to know and follow most of the laws. In his counting of the mitzvot, the Rambam concludes that nowadays there is only a difference of fourteen mitzvot between men and woman, which shows how much women need to know if they are to practice correctly. In this vein, a number of years ago, the Rebbe said that women

---

147   Midrash Tono Dbei Eliyohu Rabba Ch. 9
148   47:10

can and should learn whatever they want, even going so far as to say that women should learn Gemara or Talmud as well.[149]

Speaking of which, the Talmud states that women have a merit in the study of Torah more than men because they inspire their children and husbands to study every day.[150] This encouragement and enabling of others to study grants women a greater reward than learning Torah on their own would grant them. An example of this concept is found in the Torah with two of the twelve tribes of Israel, Yissachar and Zevulun. Yissachar was older than Zevulun, but the Torah mentions Zevulun first because of the special merit he had in financially enabling his brother to study Torah.[151] Just as Zevulun's financial support allowed Yissachar to study Torah all day, men also need the support and encouragement of their wives and mothers to study Torah. This is how women get double points when it comes to Torah study, as they study on their own and they inspire their family to learn as well.

In truth, through the span of our history, we find that women have always studied and excelled in Torah study. The Torah tells of how the Daughters of Tzelofchad asked a question that even Moses, the leader and first teacher of the Jewish people, could not answer. Their question was in regard to the laws of inheritance: when there are no sons, is a daughter able to inherit? This question was especially important to them, because the people were readying to enter the land of Israel and their father had died without leaving any sons. The sisters loved the land and wanted a portion in it, too. Not knowing the answer, Moses turned to G-d, who said that Tzelofchad's daughters spoke well and that their father's inheritance should be transferred to them. On top of all this, the entire law of inheritance was given to all of the Jewish people for all generations to come in their name.[152]

The Talmud remarks that the Daughters of Tzelofchad "were clever, intelligent and G-d fearing." The Talmud further explains that the above story shows how much the women loved the land of Israel. The decree

---

[149]   See talk of Beraishis (II) 5728 Chap. 14, #14. 15th of Shvat 5732 Ch. 4 Sefer Hasichos Emor 5750

[150]   Tractate Brochos 17A

[151]   See Rashi in Deuteronomy 33:18

[152]   Numbers 27:6-11, Tractate, Baba Basra 119B

that all those aged 20-60 would perish in the desert only pertained to the men and not the women, because these women were asking a practical question about owning a part of the land themselves. Going further, according to Halacha, women are supposed to be taken care of first. When a husband dies, his money is first designated to support his widow, then his unmarried daughters, and only after that do the sons get a piece of the remaining inheritance.

Another famous woman is found in the Book of Judges. There it describes Deborah, who was both a Judge and a warrior. Even though she was the most knowledgeable person in her generation, she never dictated rulings on the law. Rather, she only helped the rabbis formulate their discussions.[153] Furthermore, she never compromised her modesty; she only spoke to men in a public area under a date palm, so that people from all around could see her. The tree was high enough to create an open space and still provide ample shade from the scorching sun.

In regard to women and Torah study, the Talmud speaks about the epitome of a female Torah scholar, Bruriya the wife of the great Rabbi Meir, who is also credited with having taught her husband a lesson in how to pray. The story goes that Rabbi Meir had neighbors who caused him much strife and aggravation because of their disrespect toward G-d and His Torah. Rabbi Meir was ready to pray that G-d remove these evil people from the world, but Bruriya stopped him. Rabbi Meir defended his decision by quoting from Psalms that "evil will cease from the earth."[154] Bruriya responded by advising Rabbi Meir to pray that evil should end, not evil people, in that he should pray they repent from their nasty and evil ways.

Similarly, there have been women in all generations who challenged their teachers and rabbis in Halachic matters and were thereby able to influence the directions of certain decisions. Still, women did not become the deciders of the law. Today, women can and must challenge the status quo and outcome of modern Halacha, but at the same time remain faithful to tradition and not seek rabbinic posts.

---

[153] Tosafos on Gittin 88b
[154] Tractate Brachos 10a

An example in more recent times is Rochel, the grandmother of the Alter Rebbe, who was also known for her genius in Torah knowledge. Rabbi Yosef Yitzchak Schneersohn, the sixth Lubavitcher Rebbe, in his book *Memoirs* recounts the following story about her.

One Shabbat, soon after Rochel's marriage to Schneur Zalman, the family was walking home from the *Beit HaMidrash,* house of study. All were wearing gloves in honor of Shabbat, but as they lived in Posen, they did not need to stitch their gloves to their sleeves because their town was surrounded by an *eruv,* which allowed them to carry items. Rochel's brother Binyamin was carrying some books that he borrowed from the *Beit HaMidrash* to study at home. As they walked, a *shamash* or beadle suddenly ran after them calling out that the eruv had failed. They all stopped in bewilderment not knowing what they should do with their gloves and with the books that Rochel's brother had under his arm. Should they throw everything away or just remain where they were, because walking further would break the *Halacha* against carrying in public areas on Shabbat?

Rochel's father, Baruch Batlan turned to the men and remarked with a smile, "We men are so busy studying *Gemara* and other such courses of study that when we are faced with deciding practical *halacha,* we do not know it. We are therefore left with no alternative but to turn to Rochel." Turing to his daughter next he asked, "Well, Rochel, you are an expert in the laws of *Shluchan Aruch,* tell us what are we to do now?"

Rabbi Shneur Zalman, who was a great scholar and four years Rochel's senior, opened his eyes in wonderment at her father's question! Was this some sort of joke? How could a mere woman gain such knowledge? He had regarded Rochel as a fine but uneducated woman, like most others in that generation.

Rochel began to blush, she would certainly not, at this early stage in her relationship with her husband, wish to give away the secret that she was a scholar. She was by nature rather modest and reserved, but her father had put her on the spot and she knew she had to answer under the circumstances.

> *Her father had put her on the spot and she knew she had to answer under the circumstances.*

The question was actually quite an easy one for her to answer. "There is no need to take off our gloves," she ventured quietly, "for this is a case of *bedi'eved*, accidental, and there can be no likelihood that any of us will take off our gloves and carry them, for, as we are in company, it would immediately be noticed and the person reminded. As for the books, these should be transferred from hand to hand until we reach the yard of a non-Jew, where they will be transferred from the zone of 'public property' into that of 'private property.'"

None of those present knew whether Rochel had quoted the law correctly, but her father said they had no alternative but to accept her ruling in the matter. As soon as the men arrived home, they looked up the case in the *Shulchan Aruch*, and found it exactly as Rochel had stated.

In our generation as well, women study Torah and are acknowledged for their contributions. Rebbetzin Nechama Liebowitz, of blessed memory, and Rebbetzin Esther Jungreis of blessed memory, among others, are examples of women who are famous for their contributions to Torah study.

It is interesting to note that Moses was the one who instituted that the Torah should be read in public at least three days a week.[155] The intent of doing so was so that the Torah should not be forgotten by the Jewish people. In practice today, the Torah is read in synagogues all across the world on Mondays, Thursdays and Shabbat, in addition to holidays and the first day of a new month. Another objective to this practice is to spark the flame of Torah within man, woman and child. Even though women are not given an Aliya or called to the Torah in public (because of distraction as explained in the chapter on *mechitzah*), it is equally important that they study Torah and more importantly follow in its ways, as the Talmud states, "Great is the study of Torah for it brings to action."[156]

---

[155] Tractate Baba Kama 82A; Rambam, Laws of Tefilla Chapter 12 Law 1.

[156] Tractate Kiddushin 40b.

This directly connects to another issue about whether women should be called up for an *Aliyah* or dance with a Torah scroll on Simchat Torah, when we celebrate the end of the weekly Torah readings for the year and immediately begin again. On Simchat Torah, one becomes the feet of the Torah by holding it when dancing; however, leading Torah authorities of our generation have strongly objected to women carrying the Torah, among them, the Lubavitcher Rebbe, Rabbi Moses Feinstein and Rabbi J.B. Soloveitchik.

The simple reason for this is that we cannot change a tradition so entrenched that it has become like law. Our sages teach that an accepted custom among the Jewish people is authentic[157] and unshakeable. This includes customs of women as well. For example, women refrain from doing work on Chanukah while the candles are burning and they don't look at a Torah scroll if they are menstruating.[158]

Another point to consider is that just as we receive reward for study and delving into Torah, we are also granted reward for refraining from doing something we shouldn't,[159] even if our hearts strongly desire to do it. On the contrary, the Lubavitcher Rebbe says that when a woman breaches the walls of *Halacha* and tradition to get an *Aliya* (which literally means elevation) or carry the Torah, there is no greater desecration (or descent) since she is in violation of G-d's law,[160] and the Torah states one must follow the law according to the leaders of your generation.

Spirit of the Law

Metaphorically, there are two parts to every mitzvah; the body of the law and the spirit of the law. In the above case, the spirit of being called up to the Torah for an *Aliya* and carrying the Torah is to inspire us to learn more and hold the Torah dear. This aspect of the mitzvah applies equally to women and to men, as both were given the Torah by G-d on Mount Sinai. We stated earlier that women were actually asked first to accept the Torah, and only after they agreed were the men asked. Also,

---

[157] See Tractate Menochot 20b (Tosfot).
[158] Alter Rebbe's Shulchan Aruch 88:2; Appendix 5 p.150-152
[159] Talmud Pesachin 22b.
[160] Toras Menachem 5745, Vol. 1, P. 132.

it is important to reemphasize that women have an obligation to study the laws of the Torah that pertain to their role in Jewish life. Equally and even more important is for women to learn Kabbalah and Chassidus as these branches of study help increase in love and awe of G-d.

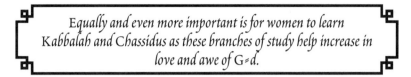

Equally and even more important is for women to learn Kabbalah and Chassidus as these branches of study help increase in love and awe of G-d.

The Rebbe also asserted that, more than men, women have a greater affinity toward the study of Chassidus. This is in line with the Talmudic teaching that a greater level of understanding was given to women than to men.[161] Tradition holds that there are fifty levels, or gates, of understanding.[162] To put this into perspective, our teacher Moses only reached the fiftieth level of understanding on the day of his passing.[163] Women today, however, can acquire it by studying Kabbalah, and even more so through the teachings of Chassidus. Perhaps this is the true *Aliya* to the Torah, to acquire the "Fiftieth Gate" of wisdom.

Another way for a woman to experience an *Aliyah* is through watching her husband get called up to the Torah for an *Aliyah*. As explained earlier, a husband and wife are two halves of the same soul, so when the husband gets an *Aliya*, the wife does, too.

The Lubavitcher Rebbe spoke of his mother Rebbetzin Chana, who as a young girl would hand copy Chassidic discourses of the Rebbe Maharash, the fourth Lubavitcher Rebbe, when they were sent from Lubavitch to her home.[164] She was also later responsible for smuggling her husband's manuscripts on Kabballah out of Russia. These manuscripts are increasingly studied by thousands of people worldwide.

On a much broader note, the Talmud states that it was in the merit of the righteous women that our forefathers were redeemed from the land of Egypt.[165] The AriZal teaches that the souls of this generation

---

[161]   Talmud Niddah 45b.

[162]   Talmud Rosh Hashana 21b.

[163]   Likkutei Torah & Sefer Halikutim of the AriZal Voeschanan 3:26.

[164]   Toras Menachem, 5749, Vol. 1, P. 45.

[165]   Midrash Yalkut Tehillim 68, Remez 795.

are reincarnations of the souls that left the land of Egypt.[166] Just like the women in that generation inspired their husbands and children to be deserving of redemption, so too is it incumbent upon all women of our generation to exercise their feminine mystique to truly inspire themselves, their spouses, and their families to prepare for the imminent arrival of the coming of Moshiach.[167] Amen.

✹ ✹ ✹ ✹ ✹

To summarize, a women can and should learn Talmud and Chassidus. If they have the capacity to teach and lead, then they must do so as well. Today, more than ever, the world needs their leadership and warmth; however, halachic decisions should be left to the Rabbis. Furthermore, for a woman to be a pulpit rabbi would simply be impossible and sacrilegious since the separation in the synagogue deems it inappropriate for a woman to lead the services or sermonize. Still, women must be continuously vigilant in challenging their spouses, children and rabbis to be more learned and creative in Torah study and spreading the law!

Story

The story of Rabbi Akiva has always intrigued me, specifically because of the role his wife Rachel played in turning him into a renowned Torah scholar.[168]

Rachel was the daughter of the wealthiest man in Jerusalem, Kalba Savua, who had big dreams for his daughter, and wanted to marry her off to the greatest and sharpest student in all of Israel. Rachel, however, declined any and all offers he brought before her. Finally her father demanded to know the reason for her rejection of some very fine suitors, and she admitted that she had her eyes on the simple shepherd Akiva. Upon hearing this, Kalba Savua vowed that if she would marry the ignorant shepherd he would withhold her dowry, disown her and refuse to support her any longer.

---

166   Shaar Hagilgulim - Introduction 20 and more.
167   Toras Menachem Yud Shvat 5717 Ch.22.
168   Tractate Nedarim 50a.

Rachel insisted that she saw greatness in Akiva, although he didn't even recognize the first letter *aleph* of the Hebrew alphabet, so she left a life of wealth and comfort and married him. With Rachel's unwavering support, Akiva went off to learn and twelve years later returned a highly regarded Torah scholar with twelve thousand students. Upon arriving at his poor and humble abode, Akiva overheard a conversation between Rachel and their neighbor.

"Aren't you excited that your husband is returning with twelve thousand students?" the neighbor giddily exclaimed.

"I am so proud of him," Rachel replied, "and if he resumed studying for another twelve years, I would be even more proud."

Rabbi Akiva did not even enter the house; he turned around, went back to the academy for another twelve years and finally returned home with twenty-four thousand students. By that time, respect for his Torah scholarship and academic brilliance was widespread, and the entire city of Jerusalem came to welcome the great Rabbi Akiva. Rachel came out as well, though poorly dressed in tattered clothing. As she approached her husband, his students tried to keep her away, unsure of what a beggarly looking woman wanted from their Rabbi.

Rabbi Akiva noticed what was taking place and gestured to his students to let her through. "All that I have learned and all that you have learned," he explained, "we owe to her."[169]

To fully highlight this point, the Talmud declares that the disciples of Rabbi Akiva saved the Torah at that time.[170] The Rebbe elaborates, "This means that the entire edifice of the Oral Torah, the very basis of the existence of our people and its ways of life, is ultimately to be credited to a Jewish Woman."[171]

---

[169] Talmud Kesubos 63a.
[170] See Talmud Yibomos 62b.
[171] From a letter of the Rebbe to the 18th Annual convention of Nshei Ubnos Chabad. Dated Lag Baomer 5733. (1973). With permission from the Kehot Publication Society.

The entire edifice of the Oral Torah, the very basis of the existence of our people and its ways of life, is ultimately to be credited to a Jewish Woman.

CHAPTER 10

Are Women Trustworthy?

Considering all the wonderful things the Torah proclaims about women, it's troubling to learn that a woman can't be called as a witness in court according to Jewish law. Why? Aren't women trustworthy?

On the contrary, if one walks into a kosher Jewish home, it is the wife who is consulted about the food. She is the one who can distinguish a dairy product from a meat product and her word is inherently trusted. If she says something is kosher, she is believed. Even though according to Torah law, the one who eats non-kosher is liable and punished with thirty nine lashes, a woman is still believed when it comes to prohibitions in Jewish law.[172]

Furthermore, in regard to *mikvah*, how does a man know if his wife truly immersed in the *mikvah*? He asks her directly and she replies that she did, because she can be trusted. And who is the one who oversees when a woman goes to the *mikvah*? How could it be a man? That would be sacrilegious! Of course, a woman attendant is on hand when another woman goes to the *mikvah* and gives a receipt to testify to this, proving that in Judaism women really can be believed.

So why is it that in areas of law pertaining to civil and capital issues women are not believed? Why don't women have a place in court proceedings?

---

[172] Talmud Pesachim 4b Tosfos Hemnuhu.

That women are not called to bear witness in court is based on the Torah verse, "On the testimony of two witnesses shall he be put to death, he shall not be put to death because of the testimony of one witness."[173] Rambam (Maimonides) explains that the Torah's use of a masculine form in the Hebrew is proof that only men can testify, not women.[174] However, this isn't satisfactory alone; it needs a sound reason to support it. The real reasoning is actually very simple.

According to Maimonides, neither a king nor a high priest can testify in court as it's beneath their dignity.[175] Imagine making a king take an oath to tell the truth and then examining and cross-examining him to prove a case. This is no way to treat a king! Similarly, a woman is given the same status as a king and high priest, which affords her a greater level of trust and respect than men. Women also have such great responsibility and have been endowed with a greater level of understanding, stemming from a higher level of sensitivity than men. This sensitivity is a blessing (as explained earlier) and consequently a woman must sensitize her spouse and children to serve G-d and study Torah with love, joy and awe. To put her under such scrutiny would be very disrespectful. This is why it states in the Code of Jewish Law that if a woman must testify we don't try to stump her.[176] We accept her testimony as a trustworthy individual.

There are court cases in which a woman does testify. For example, in the case of an *aguna*, an abandoned wife whose husband's whereabouts are unknown. If another woman testifies that the husband died, or even if the wife herself testifies to her husband's death, the *aguna* may remarry based on her own testimony.[177] When a woman testifies, her testimony carries the weight of two witnesses, the necessary minimum to establish veracity in a court of law. Thus, if after a woman testifies that a man died, and after that one witness testifies that the man didn't die, we accept the first woman's testimony because her testimony is the equivalent of two witnesses, so the widow may remarry.[178]

---

[173] Deuteronomy 17:6; 19:15
[174] Law of Edus, 9:2; see Radbaz on Rambam Ibid and Choshen Mishpat, 35:14.
[175] See laws of Edut Ch. 1:3 and 11:9 and laws of kings, Ch. 3:7, Chosen Mishpat; 28:5
[176] Code of Jewish Law, Even Ezer 17:21.
[177] Code of Jewish Law, Even Ezer 17:43.
[178] Code of Jewish Law Even Ezer 17:37

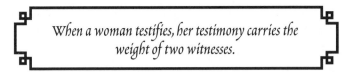

When a woman testifies, her testimony carries the weight of two witnesses.

Perhaps the most compelling answer as to why women do not testify is found in the laws regarding the cities of refuge. The Torah says that if a person kills another unintentionally, the murderer must flee to one of the forty-eight cities of refuge, which offer protection from relatives of the murdered individual's family who want to avenge his blood. The murderer may not leave the city until the death of the High Priest, or the avenger of blood is allowed to kill him. The law continues, saying that the refugee may not even leave the city to testify for a murder case, even if the refugee has information that can acquit the defendant standing trial. Furthermore, even if the refugee is as great and capable as Yoav Ben Tzruah, the general of King David, and all of Israel needs him to defend her, the refugee still may not leave. If the refugee leaves, he agreed to his own death as explained above.[179]

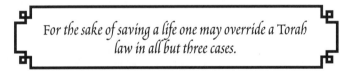

For the sake of saving a life one may override a Torah law in all but three cases.

Many commentaries try to understand what seems to be a very confusing and extreme law; for the sake of saving a life one may override a Torah law in all but three cases, (1) Idolatry (2) Adultery (3) Murdering another person. There is not even a question when it comes to breaking the laws of Shabbat in order to save a life. Furthermore, in such a case, breaking the laws is considered as honoring the Shabbat, since on the day of Shabbat you helped save a life. Why then is the refugee not allowed to override this law to save one or many lives?

The Rebbe explains that outside the city of refuge the refugee is considered to be a dead person (for he or she would surely be killed), and simply put, a dead person cannot testify or save anyone. As the Torah doesn't permit the refugee to leave, even to save a defendant's life, this is the biggest proof that the refugee will not be able to save that life and their testimony will not be beneficial. If Torah law doesn't allow the king

---

[179] Rambam, Laws of Rotzeach & Shmiras Nefesh 7:8

to leave his palace or the High Priest the Holy Temple it is because their testimony will not help. Similarly, a woman cannot leave her home, a miniature holy temple, to testify. If Jewish law dictates that she doesn't testify, it means that her testimony is not needed and salvation will surely come another way.

Bringing this concept of testimony to a new level, consider the Book of Isaiah in which G-d tells the Jewish people, "You are my witnesses."[180] The witness's objective is to reveal information that would not otherwise be known. As a people, our mission is not only to reveal that G-d created the natural universe, and that G-d is infinitely greater than the universe, but also to reveal G-d's essence, that combination of infinite and finite wrapped into one.[181]

This phenomenon was most strongly experienced in the *Mishkan* and Holy Temple. The holy mystics teach that the Holy Ark of G-d, though 2 ½ cubits in length and 1 ½ cubits in width, did not take up any space. The Ark was stored in the Holy of Holies, a room which was only 10 cubits by 10 cubits. Even after placing the Ark on the floor there were still 10 square cubits of space available.[182]

This is something that all of us, both men and women, must testify to. An easy way to start doing so is by reciting the *shema* twice daily. As stated in the Talmud, when we recite the words "Hear Oh Israel, G-d is Our G-d, G-d is One," we all testify to G-d's oneness.

Story

An *aguna*[183] once asked the Tzemach Tzedek, the third Rebbe of Lubavitch, to convene a court and receive witnesses who claimed they had witnessed her husband's death, the verification of which would allow her to remarry. The Tzemach Tzedek procrastinated on holding the court, and after some time the missing husband suddenly returned home.

---

180   Isiah 43:10
181   Sefer Hamaamarim Milukot; Ki Yishalcha.
182   Talmud Yoma 21a.
183   Literally, a chained or anchored woman, because she cannot remarry unless she received a bill of divorce or testimony to her husband's death.

When the a*guna* asked the Tzemach Tzedek why he originally refused the case he responded, "I saw [with divine providence] that your husband was still alive. If we would have accepted the testimony of these witnesses your husband would have surely died."

CHAPTER 11

Thank You G‑d for Making Me a Woman

Let's return to the original question that has been plaguing us from the start. Why, after all we've discussed about the Torah's high esteem for women, do men still make the blessing "Thank You G-d for not making me a woman"?

It's crystal clear that Judaism not only considers a woman equal to a man, but also endows her with greater qualities in many ways. Therefore, the only logical sense that we can make of the above blessing is in its deeper meaning.

There are actually two answers given to our perplexing question. One is a popular answer based on *Halacha,* the second comes from a more Kabbalistic approach.

The *Halachic* answer notes that a man has the obligation to fulfill 613 commandments, a great and awesome responsibility, so he thanks G-d for not making him a woman, who has fourteen less commandments to fulfill.[184] The blessing of "Thank You, G-d, for not making me a gentile" follows the same logic, as gentiles who only have the seven Noahide laws to fulfill. The same logic applies to the blessing of "Thank You, G-d, for not making me a servant"; the servant has more laws than a gentile, but is still not a free person and may not marry a Jew. Although stated in the negative, these blessings are actually positive affirmations of a man's humble acceptance of all the mitzvot. Even though he knows it's a difficult

---

184   Beth Yosef commentary Or Tur Ch. 46.

and tremendous task, he thanks G-d for giving him this mission and responsibility. He feels he is honored to be entrusted by G-d to fulfill the extra mitzvot. Therefore, a man is not putting a woman down through this blessing; rather, he is celebrating the great honor that because he is a man, he is able to fulfill more commandments.

This answer is good, but leaves room to wonder if there's not more to it. Even though a man should acknowledge that he can fulfill more commandments, shouldn't he only say these blessings once in his lifetime, and not every day? For example, when a boy becomes a man at the age of thirteen, he now becomes responsible for all 613 commandments, a fitting time for him to recite these blessings. Yet, men say them every day. Why?

The great Kabbalist, the holy AriZal says (and this approach is accepted by Kabbalists, and the Alter Rebbe, who brought it down in the Code of Jewish Law[185]) that these blessings have to do with the "impregnation of the soul."[186] In short, when a person goes to bed at night, a part of their soul leaves the body and goes up to Heaven, where it stands before a court of law and goes through a judgment of what it did throughout the day. The soul is then cleansed and purified and sent back down to earth refreshed, revived and ready to tackle a new day.

If a person sinned the previous day, the soul may be tormented and punished as part of the cleansing process. As the Alter Rebbe writes in Tanya[187], one of the ways is that the soul has bad dreams to purify it from any bad thoughts or sins that it committed during the day.

A worse punishment is called the "impregnation of the soul." This is when G-d attaches a foreign soul to your soul to torment and thereby purify it.

For a Jew, this could mean that his soul is impregnated with the soul of a non-Jew, or the soul of a slave. In addition, for a man it could be the impregnation of the soul of a woman.

---

[185] Code of Jewish Law by Rabbi Shneur Zalman of Liadi. Ch. 46 Law 4.
[186] See Toras Chaim Shmos 108b.
[187] Chapter 29

This explanation seems to be leaning in a more belittling direction, so what does it all really mean? Let's play it out with some basic scenarios. One morning, a person wakes up and decides, "I don't want to be Jewish today." He yanks his kippa off his head and throws it to the floor declaring, "That's it! I've had enough of this religion!" What happened? Why the change of heart? That morning a foreign soul was attached to his, possibly the soul of gentile, which wouldn't have any feeling for Judaism, so he decided he wants nothing more to do with his religion. However, that's not really the person speaking, but the voice of this extra soul he's now toting around.

Some mornings an individual wakes up feeling lethargic, overused and unwilling to go to work. Grumpily he thinks, *I don't want to work today, nobody appreciates me there. I want to quit. I just want to chill out and do nothing all day.* What happened here? It's possible that the soul of a slave attached itself to their soul. If a man gets up in the morning and decides, "I want to wear a skirt," then what happened? Maybe the soul of a woman attached herself to his.

What are we getting at? Men and women, Jews and non-Jews, each have individual roles and purposes in their lives. There is nothing degrading or belittling about the role each is born into; rather there is uniqueness to each of their creations. Men and women have different roles, so for a woman to act like a man, or a man to act like a woman, is counterproductive to their purpose, mission and goal in life. If their itinerary is switched, if each one is trying to be the other, then neither man nor woman will reach their destination.

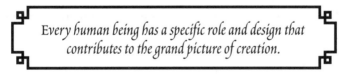

Every human being has a specific role and design that contributes to the grand picture of creation.

Therefore, the Kabbalah states that we are to say these three blessings so that a foreign soul will not attach itself to us and confuse the route to our destination. Thus, is it not a matter of one being better or worse; a Jew has his role, a non-Jew has his role, a man has his role and a woman has her role. Every human being is created in the image of G-d. Every human being is important. Every human being has a specific role and design that contributes to the grand picture of creation. This is the ultimate reason behind these blessings. They aren't derogatory, but a celebration of distinctness and individuality.

As an aside, this explanation raises an interesting question in regard to a convert to Judaism. Does a convert say the blessing, "Thank You G-d for not making me a gentile" when he was in fact born one? The answer is that a convert does recite this blessing every day, because it's not a blessing that refers to one's *origins*, but the here and now, today. When the soul returns to the body each day, it is like a person is reborn. Today I am a Jew, today I recite this blessing.

Originally, in Chapter two, we spoke about the reasoning behind dividing this part of the blessings into three instead of one, all-encompassing blessing. As we are trying to partake of as many blessings as possible each day, we break this blessing down into three to gain two extra blessings. This brings up the question: since a woman does not recite the blessing, "Thank you G-d for not making me a woman," is there something else she can say instead, so as to not miss the chance to say another blessing?

In the Kehot Prayer Book, based on the liturgy of the AriZal and compiled by the Alter Rebbe Rabbi Schneur Zalman of Liadi, it says that men recite this blessing, the specificity introducing exclusivity in that this blessing is not for women.[188] In other prayer books, it gives an alternative blessing that women should say, "Thank You, G-d, for making me according to Your will." However, the Alter Rebbe did not include this blessing in his siddur. Also, this blessing is not found in the Talmud, unlike all the other blessings in the morning liturgy.

Before continuing, it's important to note that extreme caution is taken not to change one iota of the liturgy in prayer books. Our prayers were developed by the court of Ezra the Scribe,[189] known as "The Men of the Great Assembly."[190] These 120 men were some of the greatest intellectual minds, fluent in the seventy languages of the world, and their capacity to learn and their scholarship was unmatched in the entire world. Among them were also some of the prophets, such as: Haggai, Zechariah, Malachi, Daniel, Chanania Mishael Azaryia, Nehemia and Mordechai (from the

---

[188] Page 8.
[189] Rambam Laws of Tefila 1:4.
[190] See intro to the Rambam - Yad Hachazoka.

famous story in the Megillah). In short, every word in the prayer book is holy, prophetic and purposefully placed.

The source for this "women's blessing" is traced to the fourteenth century scholar David Abud Arham, who lived many generations after "the Men of the Great Assembly." Many translate the blessing of, "Thank You, G-d, for making me according to Your will" to mean "You made us perfect. You made us according to *Your* will, not according to *our* will." In support of this, it is claimed that men need to be refined, circumcised on the eighth day, whereas for women circumcision is forbidden. The Talmud actually says that women are born circumcised.[191]

Why is this important? This all comes down to knowing when the G-dly soul enters the body. According to the Alter Rebbe in his Code of Jewish Law, the G-dly soul enters the body at the time of circumcision on the eighth day.[192] The Rebbe asserts that this specificity is also exclusivity. A woman doesn't need to wait until the eighth day for her G-dly soul to enter her body; rather, her G-dly soul entered her body at the moment of birth. Think about the age difference between a Bar and a Bat Mitvah; a Jewish boy reaches manhood at thirteen, a Jewish girl at twelve. Girls just get a head start.

When the Alter Rebbe compiled his version of the prayer book, he drew heavily from the prayer books of the holy kabbalist the AriZal and his students. As the AriZal does not include the blessing, "Thank You, G-d, for making me according to Your will," the Alter Rebbe left it out of his prayer book as well. This blessing seems quite harmless, even empowering and encouraging, so it appears odd that the Alter Rebbe wouldn't want women to say it.

In his Code of Jewish Law, the Alter Rebbe rules that women should not say this blessing.[193] According to his reasoning, reciting it sounds like justifying an evil judgment, i.e., accepting a negative judgment upon yourself. As well, saying this blessing could also translate to mean, "Ok, G-d, You made me a woman. I would rather be a man, but if this is Your will, so I accept it." The Alter Rebbe doesn't include this blessing in his prayer book because he does not think that being created a woman is

---

[191] Tractate Avoda Zara 27a.
[192] Chapter 4:2
[193] Chapter 46

something that needs to be "accepted" or apologized for. Women need not be embarrassed about their creation, and this blessing may indicate that being created a woman is somehow secondary to being created a man.

Bottom line: Women and men are equal.

Story

The Rebbe Rashab, the fifth Rebbe of Chabad, would often discuss matters of communal interests with Rav Yitzchok Yoel Raphalovitch.

The Rebbe Rashab once explained this preference by describing Rav Raphalovitch's unique talent. "Rav Yitzchok Yoel has the ability to rebut the attacks of the government ministers. His replies are solid and cannot be refuted."

One time, the Rebbe Rashab and Rav Yitzchok met with a certain minister to convince him to rescind a certain anti-Semitic decree. In the course of their discussion, the minister said, "We have the right to persecute you Jews. You despise us, and you say it so clearly every day in your morning prayers! Take a look at your prayer book. Every morning you say, 'Blessed are you G-d . . . Who has not made me a gentile.' You Jews hate us!"

Without hesitating a moment Rav Yitzchok replied, "Honored Minister, do you love your wife?" "Do I love my wife?!? I love her more than anything else. I would do anything for her!"

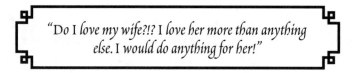

"Do I love my wife?!? I love her more than anything else. I would do anything for her!"

"We also love our wives," said Rav Yitzchok. "Yet, right after the blessing you just quoted, we say an additional blessing, 'Blessed are You G-d ...for not making me a woman.' What is the meaning of this blessing?"

Seeing that he had attracted the minister's curiosity, he continued. "A woman carries a child for nine months, has labor and birthing pains, then has the responsibility of raising children in addition to running her household. This requires a great amount of strength, endurance and patience, things that most men lack. So we thank G-d for not giving us the responsibilities of a woman."

"The same is true regarding gentiles," Rav Yitzchok concluded. "Every person, Jew or gentile, must serve his Creator. We, however, have it easy. G-d gave us 613 laws that tell us exactly what to do. A gentile was only given seven laws, and he has to figure out the rest on his own. We thank G-d for making our job easier."

Surprised by Rav Yitzchok's swift, novel response, the minister burst out laughing. He turned to the Rebbe Rashab. "You're lucky you have such a clever person with you. I am retracting my decree."[194]

---

[194] As told by Rabbi S.B. Avtzon.

CHAPTER 12

Making Circles Around Your Man

What is more important, the heart or the brain of a person? If you remove someone's heart the body cannot live, but if the brain is severed the person is dead. It's ludicrous to think that one is more important than the other.

Who is greater, the actor or the director? Without the director there is no story, without the actor there is no one on stage.

This same logic applies to men and women. Both are essential for our mission on this earth; both are mutually symbiotic and serve to compliment and complete the other. A major theme in Kabballah, and an idea very much developed by the Rebbe, is that a man and woman are only one half of a whole. At birth the soul splits, half goes into the woman, the other half into the man. The Zohar calls it "plag gufa" or half a body.[195]

> At birth the soul splits, half goes into the woman the other half into the man. The Zohar calls it "plag gufa" or half a body.

---

[195] Zohar III page 7b. 109b. 296a.

This is the reason for the great joy brought about by a wedding. Can you imagine losing your favorite watch or an expensive diamond ring? Can you imagine not seeing your parent or sibling or the love of your life for fifteen, twenty or thirty years? At a wedding two halves of a soul are reunited, which ignites a feeling akin to finding something dearly loved that was lost. Hence, the incredible joy experienced at a wedding.[196]

Why would G-d split a soul? It seems a waste to not create someone whole to begin with. In truth, G-d did not split this soul in vain, but rather to divide and conquer. From the very beginning, G-d tells Adam and Eve to be fruitful and multiply ... and conquer. As such, He gave certain responsibilities to the woman, others to the man and still others for both of them to do. For example, both women and men must "Love your friend as yourself,"[197] a commandment crucial to the vitality and survival of the nation of Israel. Another example is the mitzvah of "Knowing G-d."[198] This is not a matter of simply believing that G-d exists, but to know intellectually and logically that there is a first cause that brought and continues to bring everything in this universe into existence. This understanding must be so crystal clear as to actually recognize the energy force, G-d, who causes all things to exist. Belief and knowledge of G-d are essential for building our lives and fulfilling our purpose in this world.

There are other practices or mitzvot that are not shared as they are exclusive and unique to each sex, some of which we have already discussed. These divergences in serving G-d are better appreciated with a parable of the human body.[199] Blood unites and runs through all the limbs of the body, but each limb and organ serves a unique and distinct purpose. Blood represents the mitzvot that are unisexual. The limbs and organs, like the brain and the heart, allude to their respective roles in serving the Divine. The heart has an advantage over the brain for it is warm and passionate in contrast to the cold and calculating brain. However, the brain is objective and decisive, unlike the emotional and prejudiced heart.

---

[196] Toras Menachem 5714 vol. II page 173 footnote 2.
[197] Leviticus 9:18
[198] Rambam Laws of Yesodei Hatorah at beginning; Hayom Yom 19 Shvat.
[199] For the following see Hisvaadus - Toras Menachem 5744 vol. III page 1817.

> *Blood unites and runs through all the limbs of the body, but each limb and organ serves a unique and distinct purpose.*

Pertaining to the building of the sanctuary in the desert, we are told that the women were first to offer their donations, which were considered to be holier and loftier than those of the men.[200] And this even though the women were not obligated to donate to the sanctuary since they did not sin by building the golden calf as the men did! The women didn't just give first of their money and jewelry to build the sanctuary, but they also gave of their intellect, heart and passion. As the Torah tells us, "And every woman with the wisdom in her heart spun the yarn,"[201] and "all the women whose hearts inspired them with the skill."[202] The Torah itself, G-d's word, testifies that they participated not only monetarily but with heart, soul and intellect.

This concept is underscored when the Torah tells us about the mirrors that were donated by the women. These mirrors were tools through which the women enticed their husbands to fulfill their duties in procreation to secure the continuity of the people of Israel, while suffering slavery in Egypt. Upon seeing these donated G-d said, "These mirrors are dearer to me than all of the rest."[203] These mirrors were unsolicited gifts by the woman of Israel who wanted to show their unadulterated love for G-d.

All of this also sheds some light on the actual wedding ceremony.

First the groom enters and stands under the wedding canopy known as a *chupah*. He is usually escorted by his father holding his right arm and his future father-in-law holding his left. Some have the custom to be escorted by their father and mother.

The bride then enters, escorted by her two matrons. Counterclockwise, the bride circles her groom seven times and then stands on his right side. Once this prelude is done, the Rabbi begins the betrothal blessings. Only after all this, does the groom place the ring on his bride's finger.

---

200 Likkutei Dibburim vol. III page 1142. See Rambam Vayakhel 35:22 and more.
201 Exodus 35:26
202 Exodus 35:25
203 Exodus 38:8

As simple as the ceremony may seem, there are a few questions that it arouses. Namely, why must the bride circle the groom and not the other way around? Isn't this once again another display of male chauvinism? Why doesn't the woman give the man a ring? Why seven circles around the groom and not six or eight?

The answer lies in a verse by King Solomon: "It is the wisdom of women that build the home."[204] This means it is the wisdom and understanding that G-d has imbued into the woman that gives her the intuition and practical ability to truly design and maintain the home.

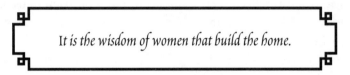

It is the wisdom of women that build the home.

Therefore, the woman is the one who circles the man seven times, because she will build the home seven days of the week for the rest of their lives. After "building" this home around her husband to be, she then enters into this home to be there with him, beside him. This circling is not because she becomes subservient to her husband; on the contrary, it's because only she can truly build this home.[205] For this reason, I often tell my congregation that it's a necessity for the wife to choose the home they live in, not the husband, for she truly understands what kind of a home is needed.

Back to the wedding ceremony. After the rituals, the Rabbi can beseech G-d's blessing to dwell in this home, for a blessing cannot manifest itself in a broken vessel. Only after the bride builds the home is the vessel complete, only then will the *shechina,* the Divine presence, come into the home.

After the bride displays her willingness to build a home with her husband to be, the man, with her consent, places a ring on her finger while saying, "You are now betrothed (holy) unto me according to the laws of Moses and Israel." To show his commitment to his wife, the husband now puts his money where his mouth is in an open display before two witnesses, whose presence make this a legally binding act. The ring shows

---

204 Proverbs 24:3
205 Teshura Tzfasman-Simpson 20 Sivan 5772 Page 11.

the husband's commitment to support his wife until the end of her days, and even after his lifetime. And this, in truth, is the real meaning of love.

Story

When Rabbi Aryeh Levine's wife, Rebbetzin Channa Tzippora, told him that she envied a certain woman neighbor, he was surprised at her remark. Why would his wife, who didn't even know what envy was, be envious of a neighbor? Who was this neighbor?

There was a wealthy man in Jerusalem whose luck had turned. His creditors latched onto everything he owned and he was forced to live in Rabbi Levine's poor neighborhood, where the dwellings were primitive, with shared bathrooms in the courtyards. To support his family, the former rich man now had to work as a day laborer, putting up scaffolding for buildings under repair.

One evening, his poor but pious neighbors were astonished to see this man's wife go out on the street in her best clothes, made up, and with her jewelry on. Then, this scene repeated itself every evening. People started to talk.

Some time later, when Rebbetzin Channa Tzippora had a conversation with this woman, things became clearer. The woman said, "My husband comes home from work every evening and his heart is about to explode. He was once so wealthy and now he's forced to work as a simple laborer. He feels humiliated, crushed. When I saw how depressed he was, I decided to put on make-up, my best clothes, and jewelry so I'd look nice for him when he comes home from work. Every evening I wait for him on Agrippas Street, to greet him with a big smile and raise his spirits."

"*I envy that woman*," said Rebbetzin Channa Tzippora. [206]

....

The bride encircles the husband - she sets the tone in the home for the husband and entire family.

---

[206] *Mikudeshet At*, P. 48.

CHAPTER 13

Chavah: The Role of Womanhood

What is the role of womanhood? I believe it all comes down to one name: *Chavah,* Eve. Chavah was the first woman in the world and was given her name because she was *em kol chai,* the mother of all life.[207] The Alter Rebbe wonders, if she is the mother of all life, why is she called Chavah? She should be called Chaya, which actually means life. Why does Adam call her ChaVah instead of ChaYa?

The Alter Rebbe answers with a revolutionary concept, which I believe is the foundation of and speaks volumes for the role and mission of women. The word *Chavah* means "to tell" or "to reveal a secret."[208] What secret is Chavah revealing? The secret of creation.

Chavah is spelled with the three Hebrew letters *chet, vav,* and *hei.* Each Hebrew letter possesses a numerical value known as a gematria, assigned to each letter in numerical order. According to this level of interpretation, the word *Chavah's* numerical equivalency is nineteen. *Chet* equals eight, *vav* equals six and *hei* equals five. Nineteen is significant because it's also the numerical equivalency of the "filled in" spelling of G-d's ineffable name.

As outlined in the following chart, the sacred name of G-d is spelled *yud,* and *hei,* and *vav* and *hei.* If you actually spell out the letter *yud* in

---

207   Genesis 3:20
208   In the verse, *vayageid,* "and Joseph told his brothers," the Aramaic commentator Onkeles translates it to mean the same as *Chavah* (Ibid 37:5).

Hebrew, it becomes *yud, vav* and *daled.* (In English, imagine spelling the letter "B" like "Bee.") The *yud* is the primary letter, whereas the *vav* and *daled* are the "filled-in" letters. The same can be done for the *hei,* and *vav,* and *hei* again of G-d's name. When you add up only the "filled-in" letters without the primary letters, the *gematria* of the letters adds up to nineteen, the same as *Chavah.*

Primary Letters Of G-d's Name	Milu Or Filled-in Letters of G-d's name	
י *Yud* (10)	ו *Vav(6)* ד *Daled(4)*	= (10)
ה *Hei* (5)	א *Alef(1)*	= (1)
ו *Vav* (6)	א *Alef(1)* ו *Vav(6)*	= (7)
ה *Hei* (5)	א *Alef (1)*	= (1)
Total = 26	Total = 19	

Simply explained, the similarities in these numerical equivalencies prove that the role of *Chavah,* of every woman in fact, is to reveal G-dliness in the world. The Kabbalah says that when G-d created the world, He concealed Himself, and that's why the world in Hebrew is called *Olam,* which means concealment. This world is a concealment of G-d; the role of every woman is to reveal it. This mission started with Chavah and has been passed on to every woman thereafter. This mission to reveal G-dliness is not designed exclusively to the macrocosm of the world, but also to the microcosm of every human being.

A woman reveals G-dliness by starting with herself, then with her spouse and her children. This is what is meant by a greater measure of understanding was given to the woman. The man biologically emits the seed, metaphorically *Chachma* on the initial stage of an idea or a concept. The woman extrapolates and elaborates by revealing and developing that seed of potential into reality, forming a viable living and sustainable organism as we explained earlier. Chavah, and every woman, in addition to inspiring their family and friends, help to cultivate and develop their spouse's and children's potential into real success and productivity.

In one word, *Chavah,* women have been endowed with the sacred ability to reveal the G-dliness that is concealed here in the world, and to reveal the potential of all human kind.

> *Women have been endowed with the sacred ability to reveal the G-dliness that is concealed here in the world, and to reveal the potential of all human kind.*

Story

In a letter to the members of N'Shei uBnos Chabad (literally "women and daughters of Chabad) worldwide, on Lag B'Omer 5723 (1983), the Rebbe relayed the following story.

Reb Gavriel was one of the most prominent Jews in Vitebsk. After twenty five years of marriage, he and his wife were childless. Then, after suffering sustained persecution, he lost all of his money, so he was very frustrated when an appeal reached him from the Alter Rebbe asking him to participate in the special mitzvah of Pidyon Shevuyim (redeeming captives). Usually, Reb Gavriel would gladly give a large contribution for this cause, which is what the Alter Rebbe was asking from him. However, his usual charity was now far beyond his present means, a point of great sadness to him.

When his wife learned of her husband's predicament, she sold her jewelry and raised the required amount. She scrubbed and polished the coins until they gleamed brightly, and with a prayer in her heart that their luck brighten too, she wrapped the coins in a bundle and gave them to her husband to send to the Alter Rebbe.

Reb Gavriel traveled to the Alter Rebbe in Liozna and placed the bundle of money on the table. The Alter Rebbe asked him to open it, revealing the coins that shone with extraordinary brilliance.

The Alter Rebbe contemplated the pile before him. Finally he said to Reb Gavriel, "Of all the gold, silver and brass that the Jews contributed to the *Mishkan* (tabernacle in the desert) nothing shone as brightly as the Laver and its stand (which were made of the brass mirrors contributed by the Jewish women with selflessness and joy). Tell me, where did you get these coins?"

Reb Gavriel reluctantly told the Rebbe about his state of affairs and how his wife, Chana Rivka bas Beila, had sold her jewelry to raise the money needed to help fulfill the mitzvah. The Alter Rebbe placed his head on his hands and fell into deep thought for a while. Then he lifted his head and bestowed Reb Gavriel and his wife the blessing of children, long life, riches and extraordinary grace. He told Reb Gavriel to close his business in Vitebsk and to begin to trade in precious gems and diamonds.

The Alter Rebbe's blessing was fulfilled. Reb Gavriel Nosei-Chein ("Gracious Gavriel") became very wealthy. He and his wife were also blessed with sons and daughters. He lived to the age of 110 years, and his wife survived him by two years.

This story fully encapsulates the role of the Jewish woman.

1. It was Chana Rivka who was first to initiate the mitzvah of charity.

2. Chana Rivka did not simply initiate and perform the mitzvah, she went beyond the call of duty by shining the coins until they sparkled. She put her heart and soul into beautifying the mitzvah.

3. She inspired the will of her husband to fulfill the mitzvah, by bringing the coins to the Alter Rebbe.

For this she brought upon her household the blessings for children, long life and prosperity.

APPENDIX I

Ten Commandments of Marriage

A book about the importance of women would not be complete without taking the time to discuss the sanctity of marriage.

There are 613 mitzvot in the Torah. The word *mitzvah* comes from the Hebrew word which means to connect.[209] Every time a Jew fulfills a mitzvah, he establishes a connection with G-d. Yet, from all 613 ways of connecting to the Divine, the only one that is specifically called *holy* is marriage, whose Hebrew word *kiddushin* actually means holiness.[210] It is only right that such a holy mitzvah should be celebrated in the best way possible. As the Previous Rebbe, Rabbi Yosef Yitzchak Schneerson, would say, "If good is good, is better not better?"

Hence, "The Ten Commandments of Marriage."

Commandment #1: COMPROMISE.

The first thing a bride and groom do when they step into their new house is kiss the *mezuzah*. The reason is because the *mezuzah* is a reminder of compromise. There are two opinions among the Sages on how a *mezuzah* should be positioned on a doorpost. One opinion says that the *mezuzah* should be vertical; the other opinion says it should be horizontal. We compromise by affixing the *mezuzah* to the doorpost diagonally.

---

209   Hayom Yom , 8 Cheshvan.
210   See Tanya Ch. 46 P. 130.

What does compromise mean? If the wife wants to go to Israel on her honeymoon, and the husband wants to go to Punta Cana, you compromise. You go to Israel.

Compromise is the first commandment of marriage.

Commandment #2: STOKE THE FIRE.

The Talmud states that *ish v'isha zachu*,[211] if man and woman are meritorious, then the Divine Spirit rests among them. Interestingly, the words *ish* (man) and *isha* (woman) contain the same letters as the word *aish* (fire). Man in Hebrew is *ish*, or fire with an additional Hebrew letter of *yud*; woman is *isha*, or fire with an additional *hei*. Therefore, if *ish* and *isha* spell out the word fire, there must be a very important message here.

In most marriages, at the very beginning the couples are on a high. They have passion, they're excited, they're in love, and then all of a sudden, a while down the road, things simmer down between them. Where did the passion go? Perhaps they wonder if they made the wrong choice, because that initial level of passion is no longer there.

Marriage is like a fire. At first, it's a big, big bonfire. There's a huge pile of wood doused in gasoline. All you need is a little match, and poof! The marriage is a blazing inferno filled with an amazingly passionate relationship. But as the fire consumes the wood, the fire dies down. The simple solution is that you have to stoke the fire. If you don't take care of the fire, if you don't keep feeding it, then it will burn down to nothing.

So how do you stoke the fire? One way is through small gestures. My wife always tells me, "Don't buy me diamonds. I'd rather you do little things; take out the garbage, buy me flowers, etc." Little things. I try to buy her flowers every Friday in honor of Shabbat, which is one of the small ways I feed the fire.

A number of years ago, I went to a local pharmacist to fill a prescription. As I was idly waiting for my order, I struck up a conversation with the man behind the counter.

---

[211] Tractate Sotah 17a.

"So tell me, how's life?" I asked.

"Ugh," he responded, "Ugh."

"Okay, so how's marriage?"

Again he replied, "Ugh."

"Marriage is 'ugh'?" I asked bewildered.

"Ugh," he repeated.

"Marriage shouldn't be 'ugh,'" I declared. "Marriage should be wow! It should be phenomenal!"

"Mine is ugh," the man said.

"Look, I'm a Rabbi," I told him, "I coach many people. Let me help you."

"Fine."

"When was the last time you bought your wife flowers?"

"I can't remember."

"When was the last time you took your wife out on a date to a restaurant?""

"I can't remember."

"When was the last time you took your wife on vacation?"

"I can't remember."

"Okay, then this is what you're going to do. Number one, you're going to buy your wife flowers once a week. Number two, you're going to go out to a restaurant once a month. Number three, you're going to go on vacation without the kids once every three months, for at least 2-3 days."

"Okay, Rabbi, when should I buy the flowers? What day of the week?"

"Well, I'm Jewish so I buy the flowers Friday before my Sabbath, but you're not Jewish, so you could buy them anytime, let's say Wednesday."

When I returned to the pharmacy the next month to refill my prescription, I asked the pharmacist, "So, how's marriage?"

"Marriage is wow! It's amazing!"

"What did you do?"

"I followed your prescription. I went across the street like you do, and bought the same kind of flowers, tulips, that you do!"

"What day of the week did you choose?"

"Well, I go on Friday."

"Why Friday, if you're not Jewish?" I asked.

"Rabbi, if it works for you, it works for me. I buy flowers on Friday. I took my wife to a restaurant, and we went on a vacation, and life is like paradise!"

I could buy my wife a beautiful diamond once every few years, or I can take the time and money to do the little things now on a more frequent basis. Buying her flowers, taking her out to eat, these are simple things that regularly enhance our marriage.

Dr. Ira Weiss, a cardiologist that treated both the Rebbe and his wife, said that the Rebbe once shared his personal regard for marriage: "The time I devote to have tea with my wife every day is as important to me as the obligation to put on *tefillin* every day."[212]

Commandment #3: RESPECT YOUR WIFE.

Thank G-d things are great, but that doesn't mean they can't get better. Unfortunately, nobody told me the following law before I got married, and I wish they would have.

The Alter Rebbe writes in his Code of Jewish Law, "*One must be very, very careful not to abuse his wife verbally, because of the fact that tears flow freely from women so G-d's wrath is swift to come [upon the husband]. And always must man be careful in the honor of his wife, for blessing is found in*

---

[212] My Encounter with the Rebbe, p.82.

his home only because of the wife, and therefore, the rabbis would tell the students of their generation, honor your wives so that you become rich.[213]

Even if you are not a halacha abiding person, you probably care about earning a living to support your family. So, honor your wife.

Commandment #4: ACCEPT IMPERFECTION.

No one is perfect… except my wife.

A woman wrote a letter to the Rebbe complaining and k'vetching, "My husband is not doing this; he is not doing that and more."

The Rebbe responded that since the sin of Adam and Eve in the Garden of Eden, there is no such thing as perfection in this world. "If you're looking for perfection, you have to wait for Moshiach to come," he explained.

This response is so amazing because it teaches us that it's okay to be *imperfect*. You're not perfect, your spouse is not perfect, and therefore, you have to let things go. A very important rule: no one in this world is perfect, accept imperfection.

Commandment #5: SAY, "YES, DEAR."

The two most important words in a marriage are: "Yes, dear." Abraham, the first Jewish man was told by G-d, "Whatever[214] your wife Sara says, hearken to her voice." This message echoes to men for all generations. Simply say, "Yes, dear."

Commandment #6: GO DAVEN (PRAY).

As equally important in a marriage as the words "Yes, dear" are the words "Go *daven*." When your husband makes you crazy, just say, "Go *daven*." Go to the synagogue and pray, get out of the house and go to the shul.

---

[213]   Code of the Jewish Law; Laws of Ono'oh & Gneivas Daat Law 32.
[214]   Genesis 21:12

Here's why:

I tell all grooms to go to the synagogue every day and *daven*, and if they can go three times a day, even better.

Their usual response is something like, "Rabbi, what's the novelty? A religious Jew should go every day and daven, right? What's that have to do with me?"

To which I respond, "Let me explain. You're getting married, and you're going to have all this passion. And it's going to be the first year of marriage, and you're very religious. You're going to follow the Torah law to the letter, and the Torah says, 'The first year of marriage, you shall make your wife happy.'[215] So you think you have to stay home all day to make your wife happy. In the morning, you're going to make her happy; in the afternoon, you're going to make her happy, in the evening, you're going to make her happy, and you're not going to go to shul. You have to go to shul, but it's more important to stay home and make your wife happy because that's what the Torah says. You can't do both at the same time. So you're not going to go to shul the whole first year.

"Shabbat comes, you make your wife happy. Sunday, you make your wife happy. Every day, happy. Three times a day, happy. All of a sudden, your wife is pregnant, and she becomes a little nauseated. It's called morning sickness. All of a sudden, she's throwing up. All of a sudden, she's not so much fun anymore. And then, all of a sudden, a baby comes. The baby is up in the middle of the night and early morning and all afternoon. You have to diaper the baby; you have to feed the baby. All of a sudden you tell your wife, 'Honey, I can't diaper the baby now. I have to *daven*.' 'Honey, I can't feed the baby right now. I have to *daven*.' 'Honey, I can't buy formula now. I have to *daven*.'

"'What do you mean you have to daven?' she'll question, wild eyed. 'Last year you were home all day. You never told me about going to *daven*. Now you've become so religious on me? You don't care about *davening*. You're just finding excuses to leave the house!'

"The way you establish yourself the first year of marriage, that is the way your life will go. If you set a precedence, 'I need to *go daven*,' not

---

[215] Deuteronomy 24:5

a problem. Go *daven*! But the moment you become over-zealous, and you're home the whole first year, you're never going to *daven* again. So '*go daven*' is a very important commandment!"

Introduction to Commandments 7, 8 & 9.

In 1963, there was a young woman who was getting married, and she went to the Rebbe for a private audience. The Rebbe asked her if she had all the things she needed for the wedding.

"Yes, of course. I have a wedding gown, I have the caterer and the wedding hall...."

"Do you have a mezuzah for your new house?" the Rebbe asked.

The lady was startled. "Yes, I have a mezuzah."

"Do you know what a mezuzah stands for?"

The woman shook her head.

"The mezuzah stands for three things," the Rebbe explained, "*Mem, Zu*, and *Zeh*."[216]

Commandment #7: STUDY TORAH TOGETHER.

The Hebrew letter *mem* has a numerical value of forty, representing the forty days and nights that Moses was on Sinai to receive the Torah. If you want to bring peace into the home, explained the Lubavitcher Rebbe, there must be Torah study in the home.

On another occasion, the Rebbe said the first thing you see when you go into a Jewish home should be Jewish books. Unfortunately, I have met many people who don't even have one Jewish book in their house. It's important that the first thing you see when you enter into a Jewish home is a *Chumash* or a Bible, a siddur or a prayer book, a *Tehillim* or the Book of Psalms, etc.

---

[216] See Kfar Chabad 1163, page 38.

A new couple must make it a priority to discuss how to bring Torah into the home, because Maimonides says that the purpose of Torah is peace.[217] G-d gave us Torah to bring peace into the world. The Mechilta teaches that G-d specifically waited to give the Torah of peace at a time when the Jewish people were at peace, as one man and one heart.[218] Only then did He proclaim, "I will give the Torah of peace to the nation of peace at the time of peace."

Therefore, it's very important that one's home is filled with Torah study and their shelves are lined with holy books.

A couple once went to the Rebbe seeking advice because they were not getting along very well.

"Did you get married *b'chuppah u'bi kiddushin*, did you get married under a chuppah?" the Rebbe asked.

"Yes," they confirmed.

"Were the seven blessings recited under the Chuppah?" the Rebbe pressed further.

"Yes."

"If you had these seven blessings, you know that G-d is with you every day of the week," the Rebbe responded. "Each blessing is for another day of the week. Therefore, these blessings give you the strength to overcome any challenge that comes in your direction."

The Rebbe then asked, "Do you study Torah together? Torah study brings peace into the home."

"What should we study?" the woman asked.

"Start with studying the portion of the week," the Rebbe instructed.

"One should take their spouse to Torah class once a week or take a holy book and put it on the table, and then start with *Bereishet*, Genesis, from the beginning, and simply discuss the words. The discussion of Torah itself will bring peace into the home.

---

[217] See Tractate Uktzin.
[218] Mechilta Yisro 19:2.

Commandment #8: THE WOMAN SETS THE TONE.

Zu, says the Talmud, represents one's wife.[219] The wife is the one that sets the tone in the house. If she wants the home to be warm, peaceful, loving, and kosher, it will be. Furthermore, she chooses the house to live in; she needs to like it and be comfortable in it. Remember it's her home, and you are lucky if she lets you inside. The Talmud states how a great Rabbi would never call his spouse, "my wife"; rather he would say, "my home." He perceived his wife to be more than a partner but rather as his whole existence and identity.

As stated already in the story of our preface, "*The Rebbe Says... it's her home*." Those unforgettable words taught me a very important lesson. It's not what the man likes about the house, because ultimately it is the woman's domain. The woman sets the tone in the home; therefore by decorating one's home with holy books, having an open home, and inviting guests in, the wife creates a home of peace and tranquility.

Commandment #9: BRING G-D INTO THE MARRIAGE.

The Hebrew word *Zeh* means "this," as seen in the biblical phrase, "This is our G-d and we will glorify Him."[220]

How do you bring G-d into a marriage? As we all know, there are three partners in a marriage: there's the husband, the wife, and the mother-in-law- I mean A-mighty G-d, of course. G-d becomes part of a marriage when you create holiness in your home. One way of doing this is through *taharat ha-mishpachah*, family purity, otherwise referred to as the laws of *mikvah*.

The objective of the *mikvah*, as the Talmud states, is literally so that the husband should desire his wife, that the wife shall be loved by her husband.[221] This is the meaning of *Zeh*- this is my G-d, and I will glorify Him.

---

219 Tractate Kesubos 67B Commenting on Deut. 15:8.
220 Exodus 15:2
221 Tractate Niddah 31b.

Commandment #10: TREAT YOUR HUSBAND LIKE A KING.

I once heard the following story from my grandfather, Rabbi Jacob J. Hecht, OBM (of blessed memory). He said that before he married my grandmother, Rebbetzin Chava Hecht, he said to her, "You should know that I'm a Yankee, and because I'm a Yankee, I will be the head of the house. If you agree to that, then we'll get married."

In her wisdom, my grandmother responded, "Yes, you can be the head, but I will be the neck. Wherever the neck turns, the head turns."

As important as it is for a husband to respect his wife, a wife must respect her husband. If a wife treats her husband like a king, he will crown her as his queen.[222] She should make him feel like the head of the house, even though she is the neck.

Maimonides states that a man should love his wife as much as himself, but respect her more than himself.[223] Marriage is a partnership, respect each other!

---

[222] Rambam Laws of Ishus 15:20.
[223] Ibid, 15:19.

APPENDIX 2

Women, the Crown of Creation[224]
A commentary on the very first letter of the Torah.

In Heaven there are two lines for husbands. The first line is for husbands who ruled over their wives during their lives. The second line is for husbands who were ruled by their wives. The second line is filled to capacity. Standing in the first line is a single fellow named Schmerel.

A few of Schmerel's earthly colleagues in the second line notice him standing alone and call out, "Eh, Schmerel, everybody knows your wife treated you like a doormat. Why are you standing in the line for husbands who ruled their wives?"

Schmerel shrugs, "Nu, what do you want from me? My wife told me to stand here."

✳✳✳✳✳

With its very first letter *bet*, the Torah ignites our curiosity. Why does the Torah, G-d's mandate to the Jewish people and the world, begin with a *bet*, which is the second letter of the Hebrew alphabet? A more logical first letter for such a holy book would have been an *alef*. Not only is *alef* the first letter of the Hebrew alphabet, but spiritually *alef* represents preeminence.

---

[224] From *By Divine Design*, pages 27-31, written by the author. Reprinted with permission.

Alef is the numeral one, alluding to G-d's Oneness. *Alef* alludes to *Alufo Shel Olam*, the Chief or Master of the World, the One Who precedes all.

Another curious phenomenon for the Torah script is that this letter *bet* is written in an enlarged font, making it stand out among all the other letters on the page. However, nothing in the Torah is ambiguous or meaningless. What, then, is the message in choosing this beginning letter, and in its size?

We could explore this letter *bet* within the framework of the passage, "G-d created the Adam ... male and female He created them."[225] Commenting on this verse, *Rashi* quotes the *Midrash:* G-d created Adam as a hermaphrodite — both genders together, a man and a woman attached back to back.

To be an *adam,*[226] a complete person, a *mentsch*, one must possess the divine qualities of both genders. One must balance the spiritual masculine and feminine energies in terms of giving versus receiving, silence versus speech, aggressiveness versus sensitivity, and abstract contemplation versus devoted commitment.

The letter *bet* expresses this inclusivity and balance in its design, numerical equivalency and in the deeper concepts it represents.

Design: Graphically,

> *the letter bet is built from two other letters: a dalet, which is a feminine letter, and below it a horizontal vav, which is a masculine letter.*

In its very design, the *bet* demonstrates the necessity of combining male and female qualities.

Gematria: *Bet* = two. This tells us that G-d created the world for two, man and woman.

---

[225] Genesis 1:27

[226] There are four different descriptive terms for "man": *adam, ish, enosh, and gever.* The most prestigious of these terms is *adam*, meaning a human being who manifests G-d's image, a truly exalted person (see Hayom Yom Entry Elul 4).

Representation: *Bereishit* or *binah*. The word *bereishit* can mean, "With the first" — meaning the first *sefirah* or attribute of consciousness, called *chochma*. *Chochmah*, original insight, is understood to be a masculine phenomenon. *Binah*, understanding or intuition, is the second *sefirah* or attribute of consciousness. *Binah* is a feminine quality.

As the Messianic Era begins to unfold, we become more conscious of the fact that the feminine mystique will be greater than that of the masculine. This is hinted to in the enigmatic phrase of King Solomon, "The woman of valor is the crown of her husband,[227]" indicating that the *woman of valor*, the feminine quality, is the crown, higher than her husband or the masculine attribute. Similarly, the Prophet Jeremiah states, "The feminine will surround (overpower) the masculine."[228]

With further evaluation, the letter *bet* seems to add an additional emphasis on the feminine. Does the Torah actually consider the feminine to be greater than the masculine?

Let's re-examine the letter.

Design: The feminine *dalet* is indeed positioned higher than the masculine *vav*, representing the superiority of the feminine mystique. Furthermore, the top of the *bet* is adorned with a crown. Because the crown is placed on the left side of the letter, the feminine side, *binah* is again emphasized. In Torah scrolls written according to Kabbalah, the *bet* of *Bereishit* has four prongs, symbolizing the Four Mothers. All of this alludes to the fact that the woman is the crown of creation.

Gematria: The woman was created second, after Adam. We can derive from this that she was an improvement upon the original human. The unusually large size of this *bet* may also suggest that the status of being the second is sometimes more important than being the first.

Representation: The Talmud says a greater level of *binah* was given to women. *Kabbalah* explains that *binah*, the feminine, actually comes from a higher source than *chochma*, the masculine. Thus, the first word of the Torah can be read *Bereishit* to mean the letter *bet* is *reishit*, first. In other words, the *bet* — the feminine mystique that

---

227 Proverbs 12:4
228 Jeremiah 31:21

is dormant in each individual — is most essential, indeed the very crown of creation.

The Rebbe stated that our mission today is to "receive the countenance of our Righteous Moshiach." He explained, "Every mitzvah we perform should be infused with the focus, 'With this mitzvah we will welcome our Righteous Moshiach.'"

> "Every mitzvah we perform should be infused with the focus, 'With this mitzvah we will welcome our Righteous Moshiach.'"

The quality of "receiving" is feminine. This sheds light on the Talmudic passage, "In the merit of the righteous women, our ancestors were redeemed from Egypt."[229] In the future Redemption we will merit the countenance of Moshiach through the essential feminine attribute of "receiving."

---

[229] Talmud Soteh 11b.

APPENDIX 3

Five Cups, Five Matriarchs
A commentary on the Passover Seder

During Passover, we express our freedom and joy by drinking of the four cups of wine. These four cups allude to the four matriarchs of Israel.[230] But how does each cup represent each woman?

SARA: The first cup of wine is called kaddeish, "to make holy." We draw holiness into the world by reciting the kiddush and proclaiming G-d as the King of the Universe. It was the matriarch, Sara (and Abraham) who had a tent that opened from all four sides, encouraging wayfarers to come in and eat. At the end of each meal, Sara would tell the guests to thank their true host and hostess, A-mighty G-d, Blessed Be His Holy Name-because it is G-d who provides us with all of our needs. Sara was kaddeish: she made the world holy.

Alternatively, kaddeish also means to separate. Sara was the first to separate from the customs and deities of her family and proclaim to the world that it is the One G-d, blessed be His Holy Name, who creates and vitalizes all of creation.

---

230   Likkutei Sichos, Vol. 26, P. 47, fn. 42; see references there.

REBECCA: The second cup is filled before the four questions, and the answers to these questions are expounded upon with the second cup. This second cup alludes to Rebecca, who was the mother, not only of Jacob, a righteous man, but also of his brother Esau, the original evil twin. Esau is the wicked son, the second son in the Haggadah. But why does the second cup, which alludes to the second son, get all the limelight and fanfare, in that most of the Haggadah is said over it?

The answer is that the second son, the *rasha*, is only bad on the outside. On the inside, he has the "echad,"[231] the G-dly spark that unites him with G-d. However, he has questions, questions about G-d and religious practices. How do you deal with him? Well, fill up a cup of wine and spend an evening or two together and discuss those questions. Questions are important. The Talmud clearly states: "A bashful student will not learn."[232] It is only through questions that one acquires new insights.

Furthermore, the entire Talmud, the basis of all Jewish law, is all about questions and answers. So Rebecca, the mother of Esau, pleads with us: If you have a wicked son who has questions, do not shun him. Embrace him, listen to his questions and give him answers.

> *If you have a wicked son who has questions, do not shun him. Embrace him, listen to his questions and give him answers.*

Rebecca lived over 3,600 years ago, yet she never gave up on her child. Although Esau was a wicked man, his mother believed in the "echad" within him. Even today, through the narrative of the Haggadah, Rebecca is talking to Esau, working to bring him home.

RACHEL: The third and fourth cups allude to Rachel and Leah. It was the custom of the Lubavitcher Rebbe to fill the cup of Elijah at the same time as the third cup and to return the wine of Elijah's cup to the bottle after drinking the fourth cup.[233] After pouring the wine into Elijah's cup, we recite, from the Haggadah: "Pour out your wrath upon the nations that do not

---

[231]   See Gutnick Haggadah.
[232]   Ethics of Our Fathers.
[233]   Sefer Hasichos 5749, P. 391.

know you."[234] This psalm is symbolic of Rachel defending her children like a loving mother. As it states, "Rachel cries for the security of her children."[235]

LEAH: G-d pouring out His wrath on the evil nations is true at the end of exile. However, in the final days, during the beginning of the Redemption, the whole world will recognize G-d and return through teshuva. The theme of return is symbolic of Leah, as it states "her eyes were dim"-she was crying, doing teshuva.

MIRIAM: Alternatively, the fifth cup, the cup of Elijah, may allude to another great matriarch and heroine of the Passover miracle: Miriam. It was Miriam who told Moses' parents that they would give birth to the redeemer of Israel,[236] and it was Miriam who sang with tambourines after the splitting of the Red Sea.[237] What Miriam was to Egypt is what Elijah is to the world today, both heralding the redemption, getting the world ready for "next year in Jerusalem."[238]

Story

There was once a wealthy couple named Elkana and Penina, who were generous to the poor and whose large house was always open to strangers. Their most valued possession was a beautiful Elijah's cup that graced their seder table each year at Passover.

Unfortunately, after some time, the wheel of fortune turned for Elkana and Penina, and they were forced to pawn all of their possessions to buy food. The only thing of value that they had left was their Elijah's cup, which they agreed never to sell, no matter how desperate they became.

One year, as Passover approached, they discovered that they did not have enough money to buy matzah, wine, or food for the seder.

"Dear Penina," said Elkana with a heavy heart, "I'm afraid we have no choice but to sell Elijah's cup."

---

[234] Psalms 79
[235] Jeremiah 31:14-16
[236] See Rashi on Exodus 2:1
[237] Exodus 15:20
[238] Verse at the end of the Haggadah.

"Never!" replied Penina, and nothing Elkana said could change her mind.

On the day before Passover, Elkana went off to study in the Beit Midrash. It pained him too much to stay at home and see the empty Elijah's cup sitting in the middle of a bare table. How sad their Passover would be this year! How could they celebrate Israel's liberation from slavery without matzah or wine?

While Elkana was gone, there was a knock on the door of his home. Penina opened it to find an elderly, well-dressed man standing before her.

"I'm a stranger in this town. May I celebrate the seders with you?"

"We have no money to buy anything for a seder this year," Penina replied sadly. "We have nothing at all in the house."

The man handed her a heavy purse. "Take this money and go buy what you need. I'll return tonight for the seder."

With a joyful heart, Penina hurried to the market and bought everything she needed for the seders. Then she ran home and prepared a great feast. When Elkana returned, Penina told him what had happened and asked him to bring their guest home with him from the synagogue that evening. But Elkana returned from the synagogue alone.

"I looked everywhere," he explained, "but there was no well-dressed stranger there."

They decided not to begin the seder until their benefactor arrived. It began to grow late and, still, there was no sign of him. At eleven o'clock, they could wait no longer, for the afikomen—the matzah consumed toward the end of the seder—must be eaten before midnight. They recited the first part of the Haggadah and then began the feast. Right after they ate the afikomen, Elkana fell asleep. But Penina stayed awake, still hoping the stranger would appear. And a short while later, when she opened the door for Elijah the Prophet, the elderly man walked in.

She ran to wake Elkana, but by the time she succeeded in arousing him from his heavy sleep, the stranger was gone. Elkana fell back to sleep, and Penina finished the Haggadah by herself.

APPENDIX 4

Yose ben Yochanan of Jerusalem said, "Let your house be open wide, let the poor be members of your household and do not gossip excessively with the women."[239] This statement was said in regard to one's own wife to emphasize how much more this should be applied to the wife of another man.

From this phrase, our Sages taught that whoever gossips excessively with the woman (one's wife):

1. Brings evil upon himself,

2. Neglects the study of Torah, and

3. In the end will inherit hell.

At first glance, this teaching seems to paint one's wife as a demon who can send a man to hell just by conversing with him too much. However, after further consideration, it is easy to see the Mishnah's unique approach to the sacred and laudable role of the woman.

---

[239] Ethics of Our Fathers. Chapter 1 Mishnah 5

First, we must understand the sequence of our Mishnah by putting it in context of the previous one. The earlier Mishnah began by stating that both Rabbis, Yose ben Yoezer and Yose ben Yochanan, received the oral tradition from their teachers.[240] As the commentaries explain, up until that point the Oral Law had been passed down by one leader of the generation to his disciple, but now it was passed down by pairs. Thus, Rabbi Yose ben Yochanan must be complimenting his colleague's teaching, which appears before his in the Mishnah.

There, Yose ben Yoezer speaks about making a home into a meeting place for Rabbis and Torah scholars, and to drink their words in with thirst. At this juncture, Rabbi Yose ben Yochanan says to Rabbi Yose ben Yoezer, "Your previous teaching refers to the role of men but what about the role of women?" We are taught that inviting guests to eat and lodge is even greater than having an audience with G-d.[241] Therefore, in addition to Torah scholarship there is an even more praiseworthy role given to the woman, to make her home a haven where poor people can acquire their sustenance.

Now a husband may feel that his wife's role is not as important as his own and that she is simply his accessory; when he is home, she must stop providing for the poor and attend to his needs unconditionally. Nonetheless, the Mishnah teaches that the man must respect his wife's role and her contribution to humanity. He is not simply to engage in idle chatter and excessive gossip with his wife, thereby pulling her away from her precious work. Rather, he must respect her role for there are needy individuals that need her attention and mental and emotional support.

This, however, is only the first part of the Mishnah, because not every husband is going to give up his wife so easily. Therefore, the Sages continue by teaching that man should know that one who speaks excessive chatter with a woman – his wife – brings evil upon himself. Why? Man and woman are truly two halves of a soul, so every good deed the wife performs the husband receives merit for as well. Thus, by being inconsiderate of his wife's role, she loses merit and her husband does, too.

---

240 Mishnah 4
241 Tractate Shabbat 126B-127A.

> *A man may argue, he simply wants his wife for himself.*

A man may argue that he is not interested in Kabbalah or souls; he simply wants his wife for himself. The Mishnah warns that the husband is also neglecting his own role to study Torah at every opportune moment. He may respond that he is not a great Torah scholar and that learning is not his thing. In response, the Mishnah maintains that in the end the husband will inherit (present tense) hell. He claims to be a practical person, but if he does not respect his wife's role and tries to diminish it, he will inherit hell on earth now!

His wife will say to him, "I see you have nothing to do, you have free time on your hands. Help me feed the poor and wounded people, help clean up after they eat, do the dishes, take out the garbage. Be productive." If her husband does not care for her role, he will inherit hell on earth.

However, men must speak and communicate with their wives about productive things such as where to educate the children, to whom to give charity and how to become more active in their community.

Such talk—the more the merrier!

APPENDIX 5

Introduction:

At the very beginning of the Rebbe's Leadership, after assuming the role of Rebbe in January of 1951, the Rebbe encouraged women to take on leadership roles. With permission from Kehot Publication Society, we present two of the many letters that the Rebbe wrote to women worldwide.

* * *

By The Grace Of G-d

12th of Adar II, 5714 (1954)

Brooklyn, NY

To Jewish Women, Mothers and Daughters-

Blessing and Greeting:

In the coming days connecting the festivals of Purim and Passover, it is incumbent upon every Jewish woman, wife, mother and daughter to reflect upon the important historical part which the Jewish woman had in these festivals, and what useful lesson may be learned therefrom.

Our law requires the Jewish woman to participate in the special mitzvot connected with the festivals of Purim and Passover (such as the Megillah, Haggadah, etc.), expressly stating that she merits these privileges because of the special merits of Jewish women in helping bring about the wonderful deliverances "in those days at this season."

As for Passover, our sages tell us at length in the Midrash that it was the Jewish women who kept up the courage and spirits of their men in the most trying times of Egyptian bondage, and who moreover raised the generations which were to receive the Torah at Sinai and later enter the Promised Land, the everlasting inheritance of our people.

The part played by Jewish women on these two occasions was somewhat different: in the case of Passover, the woman's influence was concentrated in the home and family, ("kevudah bas melech penimah"), displaying all the true feminine Jewish virtues of modesty, piety and faith. In the case of Purim, a Jewish woman showed that when Divine Providence places her in a position of prominence and influence, she uses it wholly for the benefit of her people, and is ready to sacrifice her very life for it, in compliance with the instructions of the religious authorities.

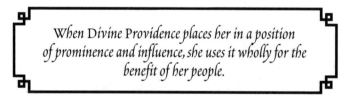

When Divine Providence places her in a position of prominence and influence, she uses it wholly for the benefit of her people.

The two festivals, Purim and Passover, are two everlasting witnesses testifying to the devotion of the Jewish woman to the Torah and mitzvot. These festivals are living testimony that, both at home and outside, the Jewish woman will do her utmost to help preserve the sacred traditions and institutions of our people, even with self-sacrifice where need be.

Jewish Women, Mothers and Daughters! Follow the example of your mothers of old and keep alive the great tradition of Jewish women. Remember, the future of our people is largely your responsibility.

Your sincere devotion to your responsibilities will surely bring you G-d's help; not only will all difficulties and dangers disappear- as in the case of Esther- but you will receive generous Divine blessings for the fulfillment of your needs and those of your family, materially and spiritually.

With blessing for a Happy Purim and a Happy and Kosher Pesach.

(signature)

Rabbi Menachem M. Schneerson

B"H

Erev Shabbat Kodesh

Vayakhel - Pikudei 5724 (1964)

Brooklyn N.Y.

To the Convention of N'shei uBnos (Woman and Daughters of) Chabad

Montreal

Blessing and Greeting:

In view of the well-known Torah expression of the Alter Rebbe, author of Tanya and Shulchan Aruch, the founder of Chabad, that "A Jew must live in accordance with the time," that is with the sedra of the week, because the Torah reflects all current events and offers the necessary instructions for day-to-day life.

The Sedra Vayakhel-Pikudei of this Shabbat, and the sedra Vayikra for next Shabbat, contain most appropriate and relevant instructions for the convention. I will dwell here on a few of these:

In Vayakhel-Pikudei the Torah tells us how the *Mishkan* with all its holy vessels was actually made, and repeats there all the details which had already been stated explicitly in [the portions of] Terumah and Tetzavah. This lengthy account, which the Torah could have foregone, emphasizes the importance of action, as our sages of blessed memory expressed it, "The deed is the most important." The earlier passages stated how G-d told Moses on Mount Sinai the whole plan of the Mishkan, while here we are told this was actually done with the personal participation of every man and woman. At the same time it is emphasized here that the women were a living example for the men ("and the men came after the women") by their sincere readiness to fulfill the Divine will.

The intended purpose of the *Mishkan* was to give concrete expression to the Divine desire and promise, "I will dwell in their midst- within each and every one." Every Jewish heart and every Jewish home should be an abode for the Divine *shechina*, just as the intended purpose of the sacrifices was that every Jewish heart come close to G-d ("an offering from you"), as the Torah emphasizes at the very beginning of Vayikra.

This expresses the eternity of the Torah. The *Mishkan* made of gold and silver, etc. can temporarily be destroyed, and the sacrifices of cattle and sheep can temporarily be suspended. The *Mishkan* in their midst and the service in their heart, however, are not affected; on the contrary, they have been strengthened. When contemplating on these teachings of the Torah at this time, each and every one must arouse in himself new strength to do everything possible to demonstrate the eternity of the Torah through living deeds in the daily life, so that the Almighty can say of each Jewish heart and every Jewish home:

"This is My Mishkan, and these prayers are My Sacrifices!"

It is the task of N'shei uBnos Chabad to help realize the aforesaid, not only with regard to themselves but also for the benefit of others, in the environment at large. That is why the A-mighty bestowed upon Jewish women a very great measure of sincere and profound feelings of *ahavat Hashem* (love of G-d), *ahavat haTorah* (love of Torah) and *ahavat yisroel* (love of Israel), and gave them the privilege to be the *akeret habayit* (foundation of the house) in every Jewish home.

May the A-mighty grant you success in your annual undertaking, and your activities throughout the year, to fulfill your far-reaching task in the fullest measure.

With blessings for success and glad tidings,

Signed: *Rabbi Menachem M. Schneerson*

Introduction:

Women should not dance with a Torah scroll on Simchat Torah. Even though the Rebbe encouraged women's leadership roles, the Rebbe was very careful not to violate Jewish laws or custom. The following letter is included with permission. Taken from The Letter and the Spirit, Vol. III.

By the Grace of G-d
13th Kislev, 5736
Brooklyn, N.Y.

Rabbi Shlomo Riskin
New York, N.Y. 10023
Shalom U'Brocho:

Pursuant to our conversation when I had the pleasure of our recent meeting, it occurred to me subsequently that a correction is called for, and since it has practical implications in *halachah,* I am sending this letter urgently.

I refer to the subject matter we discussed relative to *Simchas Torah* and *hakofos* and women's participation therein.

After I expressed my opinion on the matter, I now realize that I had overlooked an aspect of the problem which, though not specifically connected with *Simchas Torah* and *hakofos,* is nevertheless directly related to what should be the actual practice in this matter. I have in mind the *din* cited in the *Shulchan Aruch, Orach Chayim,* par. 88, referring to women in a certain circumstance relative to visiting the synagogue and to *Sefer Torah,* etc. You will note there, and at greater length in the sources cited there and in *Acharonim,* how much the *Poskim* wrestled with the problem of women's participation under such circumstances. As the *Alter Rebbe* states in his(*Rav's) Shulchan Aruch,* cit., special consideration was given to women in certain matters on the ground (*ki yi'hi'ye lohen l'itzvon godol sha'ha'kol mis'asfin v'hen ya'amdu chutz*) [*That it would cause them much*

150

distress when everyone else gathers together and they are left outside[242]]. Be it noted that the question there refers to entering the synagogue and even then, it is not enough just *l'itzvon [normal distress]* but *itzvon gadol [great distress]*.

It follows from the above that in such matters, especially in relation to *Sefer Torah,* we have no power or authority to introduce innovations; as is also evident from the lengthy discussion there and distinction between what is done at home and in the synagogue, and the like.

Hence, the practical conclusion must be not to add anything to the established practice and certainly no permission may be given to *hakofos* with a *Sefer Torah.*

I have purposely avoided the use of the word "restrictions" for, as is well known, any matter in *Torah* – which is called *Toras Chesed* – that might appear as a restriction. It is not that at all, but on the contrary, for the utmost benefit of those concerned. There is surely no need to elaborate to you on this!

In order to ease my mind that nothing undesirable in actual practice might result from the opinion I had expressed without delving in *all* aspects of the subject under discussion, I would appreciate receiving from you a confirmation of the receipt of this letter, whether by telephone or by writing.

I would like to add a further point as to how circumspect one must be in connection with Jewish customs, whether "lenient" or "strict" (*kulo* or *chumro*). Since our discussion it has bothered me, how is it that we do not find in the writings of *Gedolei Yisroel* the thoughts we discussed, as a means of involving Jews in greater devotion and love for the *Torah.* To be sure, something of that nature we find in the introduction of girls' schools in recent generations, because the darkness of the *golus* had so intensified. But this already has its precedent in previous generations in the teaching of girls on an individual basis or in small groups, though of course not on the present scale.

---

242   Woman had taken upon themselves the stringency not to gaze at a Torah during their period of menstruation, nevertheless the Rabbis had ruled that starting a week before Rosh Hashana lasting until after the holidays they would be allowed to enter a synagogue, since they were concerned that the woman would feel left out.

Similarly in the custom of candle lighting by girls before marriage, which has recently become widespread, there was this practice in many communities of different backgrounds.

Yet, in the matter of *Simchas Torah* and *hakofos,* there has nowhere been any precedent of women's actual participation, although in precisely in connection with *Simchas Torah* concessions were made, as cited in *Acharonim,* par. 669. But I realize now that the reason is simple, namely, the one cited above, but because it is not cited in connection with the laws of *Simchas Torah,* it is easily overlooked. This a case where one can indeed apply the saying of the Sages, in paraphrase: (*k'sheim she'm'kablim s'char al ha'drisha kein m'kablim s'char al ha'prisha*), [Just as one receives reward for exigence so too one receives reward for abstinence].

Needless to say, I have no objection to your quoting me in accordance with this letter, that it is a *charotto* of the previous position, for the important thing is that the actual practice should be in strict conformity with the *halachah.*

With esteem and blessing,

Rabbi Menachem M. Schneerson

APPENDIX 6

ב"ה

Abridged Daily Prayers for Women

Upon arising in the morning, place both hands together, lower your head in supplication and recite the following prayer:

1. **Modeh ani l'fönechö melech chai v'kayöm, she-heche- zartö bi nish'mösi b'chemlö, raböh emunösechö**

Translation: **I offer thanks to You, living and eternal King, for You have mercifully restored my soul within me; Your faithfulness is great.**

2. **Böruch atöh ado-nöy elo-haynu melech hö-olöm, asher böchar bönu mi-köl hö-amim, v'nösan lönu es toröso. Böruch atöh ado-nöy, nosayn ha-toröh.**

Translation: **Blessed are You, L-rd our G-d, King of the universe, who chose us from all the nations, and gave us His Torah. Blessed are You, Lord, who gives the Torah.**

3. Y'vörech'chö ado-nöy V'yish-m'rechö. Yö-ayr ado-nöy pönöv ay-lechö vi-chunekö. Yisö ado-nöy pönöv aylechö V'yösaym l'chö shölom.

Translation: **May G-d bless you and safeguard you. May G-d illuminate His countenance to you and be gracious to you. May G-d turn His countenance to you and establish peace for you.**

4. Ha-rayni m'kabayl ölai mitzvas asai shel v'öhavtö l'ray-achö kö-mochö.

Translation: **I hereby undertake to fulfill the positive commandment, Love your fellow as yourself.**

5. Place your right hand over your eyes and recite: **Sh'ma yisrö-ayl, ado-nöy elo-haynu, ado-nöy echöd.** Remove hand and recite the following in an undertone: **Böruch shaym k'vod Mal'chuso l'olöm vö-ed.**

Translation: Place your right hand over your eyes and recite: **Hear, O Israel, the L-rd is our G-d, the L-rd is One.** Remove hand and recite the following in an undertone: **Blessed be the name of the glory of His kingdom forever and ever.**

6. Tzorchei amchö yisroel merubim v'daatom k'tzorö. y'hee rötzon milfone'chö Ado-nöy Elo-hainu sheteetain l'chol echod v'echod k'day parnososoi ul'chol g'viyö ug'viyö dai machsayrö, v'hatoiv b'einechö ah-say, boruch atö Ado-nöy shomaya t'filah

Translation: **The needs of your people Israel are numerous and their knowledge is scant, may it be your will G-d our G-d that you give each and every one enough for their livelihood, and to restore to each and every physical body that which they lack and actualize that which is good in your eyes. Blessed are you G-d who hears our prayer**

7. Ach tzadikim yodu lish'mechö yay-sh'vu y'shörim es pönechö.

Translation: **Indeed, the righteous will thankfully acknowledge Your name; the upright will dwell in Your presence.**

8. Recite Ad Massai (3x)

Translation: **Until when (Recite 3x)**

After Blessings for Wine, Selected Fruits, Cakes and Crackers.

Böruch atöh ado-nöy, elo-haynu melech hö-olöm (After foods prepared from the five grains:) al ha-mich- yöh

v'al ha-kalkölöh (After wine:) (v')al ha-gefen v'al p'ri ha-gefen (After grapes, figs, pomegranates, olives or dates:)

(v')al hö-aytz v'al p'ri hö-aytz: v'al t'nuvas ha-sö- deh v'al eretz chemdöh tovöh

ur'chövöh sherö-tzisö v'hin-chaltö la-avosaynu le-echol mipir-yöh v'lisbo-a mi-tuvöh,

rachem nö ado-nöy elo-haynu al yisrö-ayl amechö v'al y'rushöla-yim irechö v'al tziyon

mishkan k'vodechö v'al miz-b'chechö v'al hay-chölechö uv'nay y'rushöla-yim ir ha-

kodesh bim'hayröh v'yömaynu v'ha-alaynu l'sochöh, v'sam'chaynu vöh un'vörech'chö

bi'kdushö uv'töhöröh, (On Shabbat:) ur'tzay v'hachali-tzaynu b'yom ha-shabös ha-zeh, (On Rosh

Chodesh, Festivals, and Chol HaMoed:) v'zöch'raynu l'tovöh b'yom (On Rosh Chodesh:) rosh ha-chodesh ha-zeh,

(On Rosh Hashana:) ha-ziköron ha-zeh, (On Pesach:) chag ha-matzos ha-zeh, (On Shavuot:) chag ha-shövu-

os ha-zeh, (On Sukkot:) chag ha-sukkos ha-zeh, (On Shmini Atzeret and Simchat Torah:) Sh'mini atzeres ha-

chag ha-zeh: Ki atöh ado-nöy tov umaytiv la-kol v'no-deh l'chö al hö-öretz (After foods prepared from the five grains:) v'al ha-michyöh. (After wine:) v'al p'ri ha-göfen. (After grapes, figs, pomegranates, olives or dates:) v'al

ha-payros: Böruch atöh ado-nöy, al hö-öretz (After foods prepared from the five grains:) v'al ha-mich- yöh.

(After wine:) v'al p'ri ha-göfen. (After grapes, figs, pomegranates, olives or dates:) v'al ha-payros.

Blessed are You, L-rd our G-d, King of the universe If one ate the food from five grains: **for the food and for the sustenance** If one drank wine or grape juice: **for the vine and for the fruit of grapevine** If one ate grapes, figs, pomegranates, olives or dates: **for the trees and for the fruit of the trees: And for the produce of the field and for the fine, fertile and grate Land, that You have given our fathers as inheritance to eat of its crop and to be sated with its goodness. Be merciful L-rd our G-d on Israel, your people, and on Jerusalem your city and on the mount Zion, the place of Your glory, and on the Altar and on your Temple. And reconstruct Jerusalem the Holy City speedily in our days and bring us there and gladden us with its rebuilding and we will bless You for it in holiness and purity:** On Shabbat add: **and accept favorably and console us on this day of Shabbat** On Rosh Chodesh add: **and remember us on this day of the new moon** On Rosh Hashana add: **and remember us on this day of Remembrance** On holidays and Chol Hamoed add: **also gladden us on this day of the** Pesach: **festival of Matzot** Shavuot: **festival of Shavuot** Sukkot: **festival of Sukkot** Shmini Atzeret: **festival of Shmini Atzeret: For You L-rd are good and do good to all, and we will bless You for the land and** After five grains: **for the food** After wine or grape juice: **for the fruit of vine** After five fruits: **for the fruits: Blessed are You, L-rd, for the land and** After five grains: **for the food** After wine or grape juice: **for the fruit of grapevine** After five fruits: **for the fruits**

When leaving a lavatory

Böruch atöh adonöy elohaynu melech hö-olöm, asher yötzar es hö-ö- döm b'chöchmöh,

uvörö vo n'kövim n'kövim, cha-lulim cha-lulim, göluy v'yödu-a lif'nay chisay

ch'vodechö, she-im yisösaym echöd may-hem, o im yi-pösay- ach echöd may-hem, ee

efshar l'hiska-yaym afilu shö-öh echös. Böruch atöh adonöy, rofay chöl bösör umafli

la-asos.

Blessed are You, L-rd, our G-d, sovereign of the universe, who formed humans with wisdom and created within him many openings and many hollows. It is obvious in the presence of your glorious throne that if one of them were to be blocked, or if one of them were to be opened, it would be impossible to exist even for a short while. Blessed are You, L-rd, who heals all flesh and performs wonders.

APPENDIX 7

The Seven Noachide Laws: G‑d's Laws for all Humanity

When Moses stood on Mount Sinai, G-d commanded him to teach the Noahide Laws to all nations. By living these laws, one brings peace and blessing upon oneself, one's family, and ultimately humankind. Women, as teachers and leaders, you should study them well and teach them to all of your friends and neighbors.

1. **The prohibition of idolatry**

2. **The prohibition of blasphemy**

3. **The prohibition of murder**

4. **The prohibition of immorality and promiscuity**

5. **The prohibition of theft**

6. **The establishment of a judicial system**

7. **The prohibition of cruelty to animals.**

In addition to the above, practice the giving of CHARITY and acts of goodness and kindness.

INDEX

ABOUT THE AUTHOR

Rabbi Aaron Leib Raskin was born in Brooklyn, New York, and attended the United Lubavitcher Yeshivah. He graduated from the Rabbinical College of America in 1986. A Chabad-Lubavitch emissary, Rabbi Raskin helped found Congregation B'nai Avraham of Brooklyn Heights in 1988, where he is the spiritual leader.

His weekly classes are popular with local judges, lawyers, doctors and laypeople. He has presented over 300 lectures on Jewish.tv viewed by thousands the world over. His books include: Letters of Light: A Mystical Journey Through The Hebrew Alphabet, By Divine Design : The Kabbalah of Large, Small, and Missing Letters in the Parshah, and with Thomas D. Zweifel, Rabbi Raskin co-authored The Rabbi and the CEO: The Ten Commandments for 21st Century Leaders. His speaking topics include Judaism, Women in Leadership, Teachings of the Torah, How to Be a G-dly Leader in the 21st Century, Kabbalah and Women, and Numerology and Kabbalah of the Hebrew Alphabet . Rabbi Raskin lives with his wife Shternie and their six children in Brooklyn.

Find Rabbi Raskin on Facebook, Twitter, LinkedIn, and YouTube and at www.Rabbiraskinbooks.com